a b c d e f
z g
y h
x i
w j
v k
u l
t m
s r q p o n

BEGINNING WRITERS MANUAL

Spelling Checker, Grammar Rules & Suggested Topics

2nd Edition

by Edward Fry, Ph.D.
Professor Emeritus
Rutgers University
&
Elizabeth Sakiey, Ed.D.
Professor of Reading
Rowan College of N.J.

Laguna Beach Educational Books
245 Grandview, Laguna Beach, CA 92651
Ph: 714/494-4225   Fax: 714/494-2403

BEGINNING WRITERS MANUAL
Spelling Checker, Grammar Rules & Suggested Topics

Laguna Beach Educational Books
245 Grandview
Laguna Beach, CA 92651
Ph: (714) 494-4225 Fax: (714) 494-2403

Published by Laguna Beach Educational Books
Copyright ©1995 by Edward Fry
Printed in the United States of America
by Media Lithographics, Los Angeles, CA
Edited by Reta Holmback
Typography by Andrea Wallace

ISBN   0-87673-024-1
Library of Congress Catalogue Card No. 93-077209

TABLE OF CONTENTS

Table of Contents

INTRODUCTION

This little manual is intended to assist beginning writers, be they students in elementary or secondary school or adults.

Some schools will have one for every student, some will have a smaller classroom set, others will just have one for each teacher or tutor. The manual can also be useful in the home for student's homework or the writing of any adult who wants a quick reference to common spellings and basic usage rules.

Spelling Check

The first and major portion of this book is a list of nearly 7,000 common words used in writing that can be used to check spelling. It is much faster to use this list than a dictionary because there are many words on a page and because the common variants (like irregular plurals, participle, and adjective forms) are listed under the root word. For example, do you spell the participle of "run" as "runing" or "running"? There are Spelling Rules in the appendix that will give you some guidance, but it might be faster and easier for beginning writers to just look up the correct spelling in the word list.

A second feature of the spell check word list is that it has two letter subheads. If the student knows only the first two letters, he or she will find a relatively short list of words alphabetically arranged under the subhead. For example under RU will be "rub", "rude", "rule", and "ruler", plus others.

The words selected are from a scientifically determined list of 3,000 words (a frequency count) and their common variants, plus author-selected common words from the Random House School Dictionary. It certainly isn't all the words needed by a beginning writer, but it will be over 95% of the words used by any writer of any age. Additional words needed will be Proper Nouns (like "Chicago"), words specific to some subject (like "biopsy"), and advanced literary words (like "sardonic").

Homophones are also listed in the spell checker word list. For example, "write" and "right" are both listed with brief definitions for both entries.

Suffixes

Many of the words in the Spelling Checker accept regular endings (suffixes), and you simply add them to the root word without changing the spelling of the root or the suffix. Here are the most common regular suffixes:

-s	-er	-ful
-ed	-est	-less
-ing	-ly	-ness

Most of the words (exceptions) that require a change in spelling for the root or the suffix are spelled out in the Spelling Checker list. Exceptions include doubling the final consonant before adding the suffix (ex. running) or using "es" instead of just "s" to form some plurals. See Spelling Rules for more information.

There are a number of other less common endings which can be added to many of the base words. We don't intend to include every possible variant (inflected) form, just the most common. When adding these endings, they are often just added; but for exceptions or different spellings, see the Spelling Rules in the appendix. Here are some of the less common endings:

-ion	-ate	-ability	-ial	-ary
-ive	-al	-ince	-ment	-ance
-ous	-able	-entail	-ory	

For the convenience of the user, at the bottom of every fourth page in the Spelling Checker you will find the following footnote:

Regular endings - just add to root word		
-s	-er	-ful
-ed	-est	-less
-ing	-ly	-ness
Most exceptions and root changes are listed.		

Hence, the user should first look up the root word in the spelling checker. If the user needs a variant form using a regular ending, it should just be added. If the root or ending is spelled differently, it will be listed under the root word.

Prefixes

Prefixes are much less complicated than suffixes. In nearly every case the prefix is just added to the root word without any change in spelling. Here are a few of the most common prefixes:

un-	re-	in- (im-)	sub-

dis-	en- (em-)	non-	pre-
into-	over-	mis-	inter-

The user who is concerned with words using any of these prefixes can just look up the spelling of the root word in the Spelling Checker list and add the prefix needed. Don't change the root – that is why "misspell" has two "s's".

Spelling Rules

Traditional spelling rules are not a lot of help for most writers. Mostly they have to do with the addition of suffixes. For example, if the word ends in "X", the plural is formed by "ES", not just an "S". This and a few other rules are found at the end of the Spelling Checker (see page 67).

Somewhat more helpful are spelling rules related to phonics because when most writers try to spell an unknown word, they usually use some type of phonics. The Spelling Using Phonics Charts will make this phonetic spelling more accurate. But as you probably already know, there are a lot of words that can be spelled correctly according to phonics rules that are not correct according to the dictionary (correct usage).

Closely related to these spelling rules are the sections on Capitalization, Punctuation, and Abbreviations.

Grammar

This manual does not attempt to be a complete grammar book, but it does contain some grammar basics; most important are the sections on Sentences, Verbs and Parts of Speech.

Types and Uses of Writing

This section lists a number of uses of writing, then illustrates some of the forms needed for letter writing and book reports. It also contains some information on keeping a journal, making graphs, and improving your vocabulary.

The Writing Process

The writing process is something that teachers talk about often, but it is something that even mature writers follow almost intuitively. If you are not a mature writer, follow these steps and it will help you. The last stage in improving your writing is proofreading to correct your own errors. When you are correcting someone else's errors or when someone else is correcting your writing, it is convenient to use proofreading symbols – so we have a page full of the most common proofreading symbols for you.

Story Starters

Story starters have been interesting opening sentences for a story, just to get reluctant writers started. For example: "If I won a million dollars...."

However, the story starter concept has been expanded to suggested titles, story enders, and great questions, all of which should produce some interesting story writing ideas.

Jazz Up Your Writing (Literary Terms)

This is an interesting section. Some of the literary terms used are rather obscure or unknown to many writers; but if you read the description and examples, most of these ideas will be recognizable.

You can study them one at a time and then learn more about them by trying to use them in a trial paragraph or a story that you are writing. Or you can just pick out one or two and insert them into an already existing story to see how it might be improved.

Personal Spelling List

Finally, there is a useful little section called your Personal Spelling List. This is to encourage all beginning writers, or even more experienced writers, to keep a list of words that they have had to look up. This serves two purposes: (1) it will help the writer to learn the correct spelling of the word, and (2) it will provide a handy reference to quickly look up words that you need.

Don't be embarrassed to write even common words in your personal spelling list. Everybody has certain words that present continual difficulty.

In Conclusion

Now a final comment: please take just a few minutes and turn every page in each of these sections in the latter half of the book. It will give you a review and overview. And it will make this book much more useful to you.

a

a

ab

ability
  abilities
able
  abler
  ablest
  ably
aboard
about
above
absent
absorb

ac

accent
accept *(to receive)*
  [except *(to exclude)*]
accident
  accidental
accommodate
  accommodated
  accommodating
accompany
  accompanied
  accompanies
  accompaniment
account
  accountant
accurate
  accuracy
ache
  ached
  aching
achieve
  achieved
  achiever
  achieving
  achievement
acid
acorn
acre
acrobat
  acrobatic
across
act
  actor
  actress
  action

active
activity
activities
actual

ad

ad *(advertisement)*
  [add *(find the sum)*
adapt
add *(find the sum)*
  [ad *(advertisement)*]
  adds *(combines)*
  [ads *(advertisements)*]
  [adz *(ax-like tool)*]
addition
  additional
addend
  addenda
addict
address
adjective
adjust
admire
administer
  administration
  administrator
admit
  admitted
  admitting
  admission
adopt
  adoption
ads *(advertisement)*
  [adds *(combines)*]
  [adz *(ax-like tool)*]
adult
advance
  advanced
  advancer
  advancing
advantage
adventure
  adventured
  adventurer
  adventuring
  adventuresome
  adventurous
adverb
advice
adz *(ax-like tool)*
  [adds *(combines)*]
  [ads *(advertisement)*]

af

affair
affect *(act on)*
  [effect *(something produced)*]
  affection
afford
afraid
Africa
  African
after
afternoon
afterward

ag

again
against
age
  aged
  aging
agent
ago
aggravate *(made worse)*
  [agitate *(stir up)*]
agree
  agreed
  agreement
agriculture
  agricultural
  agriculturally

ah

ah
ahead

ai

aid *(help)*
  [aide *(assistant)*]
ail *(be sick)*
  [ale *(beverage)*]
aim
air *(what you breathe)*
  [heir *(successor)*]
airplane
airport

9

aisle *(narrow path)*
  [I'll *(I will)*]
  [isle *(island)*]

al

Alabama
alarm
Alaska
  Alaskan
alcohol
  alcoholic
ale *(beverage)*
  [ail *(be sick)*]
alike
alive
all *(everything)*
  [awl *(pointed tool)*]
alley
alligator
allow
  [allowed
  (permitted)]
  [aloud *(audible)*]
ally
  allied
  allies
  allying
almost
alone
along
aloud *(audible)*
  [allowed *(permitted)*]
alphabet
  alphabetic
  alphabetical
already *(previously)*
  [all ready *(completely
  prepared or ready)*]
also
altar *(raised church table)*
  [alter *(change)*]
although
altitude
altogether *(completely)*
  [all together *(in a
  group)*
aluminum
always

am

am *(irreg. vb)*
amaze
  amazed
  amazing
America
  American
among
amount
amuse
  amused
  amusing

an

an
ancestor
anchor
ancient
and
angel
anger
angle
  angled
  angler
  angling
angry
  angrier
  angrily
animal
announce
  announced
  announcer
  announcing
annoy
annual
another
answer
ant *(insect)*
  [aunt *(parent's sister)*]
anxious
any
anybody
anyone
anything
anyway *(adverb)*
  [any way *(adjective
  and noun)*]
anywhere

ap

apart
apartment
apology
apostrophe
apparent
appeal
appear
  appearance
apple
apply
  applied
  applier
  applies
appoint
  appointee
approach
  approaches
appropriate
approve
approximate
  approximated
April
apron

ar

Arab
  Arabian
  Arabic
arc *(arched curve)*
  [ark *(a boat)*]
arch
Arctic
are *(irreg. vb)*
area
aren't *(are not)*
Argentina
argue
argument
  argumentative
arithmetic
Arizona
ark *(a boat)*
  [arc *(arched
  curve)*]
Arkansas
arm

The following regular endings are not in the word list & can be added to the root word without changes: -s -ed -ing -er -est -ly -ful -less -ness. Most exceptions & root changes are in the list.

army
   armies
around
arrange
   arranged
   arranger
   arranging
   arrangement
arrive
   arrival
   arrived
   arriving
arrow
art
article
artist
   artistic
   artistically

as

as
ascend
   acension
   ascent (a climb)
   [assent (agree)]
ash
   ashes
Asia
   Asian
aside
ask
asleep
assemble
assembly
   assemblies
assent (agree)
   [ascent (a climb)]
assistance (help)
   [assistants (those who help)]
associate
   associated
   associating
   association
assume
   assumed
   assuming
astronaut
astonomer
astronomical

at

at
ate (did eat)
   [eight (the number 8)]
Atlantic
atmosphere
   atmospheric
atom
   atomic
attach
   attaches
attack
attempt
attend
   attendance (being present)
   [attendants (escorts)]
attention
attitude
attract
attractive

au

audience
August
aunt (parent's sister)
   [ant (insect)]
aural (of the ears)
   [oral (by way of mouth)]
Australia
   Australian
Austria
   Austrian
autoharp
author
authority
   authorities
automatic
   automatically
automation
automobile
autonomy
   autonomous
autumn
   autumnal
auxiliary
   auxiliaries

av

avail
   available
   availability
average
   averaged
   averaging
avocation
avoid
   avoidable

aw

awake (irreg. vb)
   awaking
aware
   awareness
away (gone)
   [aweigh (to clear anchor)]
awesome
awful (terrible)
   [offal (entrails)]
   awfully
awl (a tool)
   [all (everything)]

ax

ax
   axes
axis
axle

ay

aye (yes)
   [eye (organ of sight)
   [I (myself)]

ba

baby
  babied
  babies
back
background
backward
bacon
bacteria
  bacterial
bad
bag
  bagged
  bagger
  bagging
bail (*scoop out water*)
  [bale (*bundle*)]
bait (*lure*)
  [bate (*lessen*)]
bake
  baked
  baker
  baking
bakery
  bakeries
balance
  balanced
  balancer
  balancing
bale (*bundle*)
  [bail (*scoop out water*)]
ball (*round object*)
  [bawl (*to cry*)]
ballet
ballgame
balloon
Baltimore
banana
band (*united group*)
  [banned (*forbidden*)]
bandage
  bandaged
  bandaging
bang
bank
banned (*forbidden*)

[band (*united group*)]
bar
  barred (*shut out*)
  [bard (*a poet*)]
  barring
bard (*a poet*)
  [barred (*shut out*)]
bare (*nude*)
  [bear (*an animal*)]
  bared
  baring (*uncovering*)
  [bearing (*manner of acting*)]
bark
barn
barrel
base (*bottom of a structure*)
  [bass (*lowest voice*)]
  based
  bases (*more than one base*)
  [basis (*foundation*)]
  basing
baseball
basic
basin
basis (*foundation*)
  bases (*more than one base*)
basket
basketball
bass (*lowest voice*)
  [base (*bottom of a structure*)]
bat
  batted
  batter
  batting
bate (*lessen*)
  [bait (*lure*)]
bath
batter
battery
  batteries
battle
  battled
  battler
  battling

bawl (*to cry*)
  [ball (*round object*)]
bay

be

be (*exist*)
  [bee (*an insect*)]
beach (*shore*)
  [beech (*type of tree*)]
  beaches
bead
beam
bean
bear (*an animal*)
  [bare (*nude*)]
  bearing (*manner of acting*)
  [baring (*uncovering*)]
  beast
beat (*whip*) (*irreg. vb*)
  [beet (*type of vegetable*)]
  beating
beau (*boyfriend*)
  [bow (*decorative knot*)]
beauty
  beauties
  beautiful
beaver
became
because
become
  becoming
bed
  bedded
  bedding
bedroom

The following regular endings are not in the word list & can be added to the root word without changes: -s -ed -ing -er -est -ly -ful -less -ness. Most exceptions & root changes are in the list.

bee (an insect)
[be (exist)]
beech (type of tree)
[beach (shore)]
beef
been (used to be)
[bin (a box)]
beep
beer (a drink)
[bier (a coffin)]
beet (type of vegetable)
[beat (whip)]
beetle
before
beg
  begged
  begging
  beggar
began
begin (irreg. vb)
  beginning
begun
behalf
behave
  behaved
  behaving
behavior
  behavioral
behind
being
Belgium
belief
believable
believe
  believed
  believer
  believing
bell (something you ring)
[belle (pretty girl)]
belly
belong
below
belt
bench
  benches
bend (irreg. vb)
beneath
benefit
bent
berry (type of fruit)
[bury (put in ground)]
  berries

berth (place to sleep)
[birth (being born)]
beside
best
bet (irreg. vb)
  betting
  bettor
betray
better (more good)
[bettor (one who bets)]
between
beyond

bi

Bible
bicycle
  bicycled
  bicycling
bid
bier (coffin)
[beer (a drink)]
big
  bigger
  biggest
  bigness
bike
bill
  billed (did bill)
  [build (construct)]
billion
bin (a box)
[been (used to be)]
biology
bird
birth (being born)
  [berth (a place to sleep)]
birthday
bit
bite (irreg. vb)
  biting
bitter
bizarre

bl

blab
black
  blacken
  blackish
blade
blame

blamed
blaming
blank
blanket
blast
blaze
  blazed
  blazing
bled
bleed (irreg. vb)
blend
blew (did blow)
[blue (a color)]
blind
blink
block
blood
  bloody
  bloodied
  bloodier
  bloodies
  bloodiest
bloom
blossom
blouse
blow
  blew (did blow)
  [blue (a color)]
blue (a color)
  [blew (did blow)]
bluff

bo

boar (pig)
[bore (uninteresting)]
board (1. plank, 2. get on)
[bored (uninterested)]
boarder (one who boards)
[border (boundary)]
boat
body
  bodies

boil
bold
  bolder *(more bold)*
  [boulder *(big stone)*]
Bolivia
boll *(cotton pod)*
  [bowl *(1. a dish, 2. play tenpins)*]
bond
bone
  boned
  boning
bonnet
bonus
boo
book
bookkeeper
boom
boost
boot
border *(boundary)*
  [boarder *(one who boards)*]
bore *(uninteresting)*
  [boar *(pig)*]
  bored *(uninterested)*
  [board *(1. plank, 2. get on)*]
born *(delivered at birth)*
  [borne *(carried)*]
borough *(part of a city)*
  [burro *(donkey)*]
  [burrow *(to dig)*]
borrow
boss
  bossy
Boston
  Bostonian
both
bother
bottle
  bottled
  bottler
  bottling
bottom
bough *(limb of a tree)*
  [bow *(front end of a ship)*]
bought

bouillon *(clear broth)*
  [bullion *(uncoined gold or silver)*]
boulder *(a large rock)*
  [bolder *(more bold)*]
bounce
bound
boundary
  boundaries
bow *(decorating knot)*
  [beau *(boyfriend)*]
bow *(front end of a ship)*
  [bough *(limb of a tree)*]
bowl *(1. dish, 2. play tenpins)*
  [boll *(cotton pod)*]
box
  boxes
boy *(male child)*
  [buoy *(floating marker)*]

br

bracelet
brag
brain
  brainy
brake *(device for stopping vehicles)*
  [break *(take apart by force)*]
  braked
  braking
branch
  branches
brand
brass
  brasses
  brassy
brave
  braved
  braver
  bravest
  braving
Brazil
  Brazilian
bread *(food)*
  [bred *(raised)*]

break *(take apart by force) (irreg. vb)*
  [brake *(device for stopping vehicles)*]
breakfast
breath
breathe
  breathable
  breathed
  breather
  breathing
bred *(raised)*
  [bread *(food)*]
breeze
  breezed
  breezing
brew
brewed *(boiled)*
  [brood *(group of offspring)*]
brews *(boils)*
  [bruise *(an injury)*]
brick
bridal *(relating to a bride)*
  [bridle *(part of a horse harness)*]
bridge
  bridged
  bridging
bridle *(part of a horse harness)*
  [bridal *(relating to a bride)*]
brief
bright
brilliant
bring *(irreg. vb)*
Britain
  British
broad
broke
  broken
brood *(group of offspring)*
  [brewed *(boiled)*]
brook
brother
brought
brown
bruise *(an injury)*

The following regular endings are not in the word list & can be added to the root word without changes: -s -ed -ing -er -est -ly -ful -less -ness. Most exceptions & root changes are in the list.

[brews *(boils)*]
brush
  brushes

bu

bubble
  bubbled
  bubbling
  bubbly
buck
bucket
bud
  budded
  budding
buffalo
  buffaloes
bug
build *(construct) (irreg. vb)*
  [billed *(did bill)*]
built
bulb
Bulgaria
bull
bullet
bullion *(uncoined gold or silver)*
  [bouillon *(clear broth)*]
bump
bunch
  bunches
bundle
  bundled
  bundling
buoy *(floating marker)*
  [boy *(male child)*]
burn
burro *(donkey)*
  [borough *(part of a city)*]
  [burrow *(to dig)*]
burst *(irreg. vb)*
bury *(put in ground)*
  [berry *(type of fruit)*]
bus
  buses
bush
  bushes
bushy

bushier
bushiest
bushiness
business
  businesses
bust
busy
  busied
  busier
  busiest
  busily
but *(except)*
  [butt *(the hindmost end)*]
butter
buttery
butterfly
  butterflies
button
buy *(purchase) (irreg. vb)*
  [by *(beside)*]
  [bye *(farewell)*]

by

by *(beside)*
  [buy *(purchase)*]
  [bye *(farewell)*]

ca

cabbage
cabin
cabinet
cache *(hiding place for goods)*
  [cash *(money)*]
cage
  caged
  caging
cake
  caked
  caking
calf
  calves
California
  Californian
call
callous *(unfeeling)*
  [callus *(hardened skin tissue)*]

calm
came
camel
camera
camp
campaign
can
  canned
  canner
  canning
Canada
  Canadian
canal
candle
candy
  candied
  candies
cane
cannon *(large military gun)*
  [canon *(law)*]
can't *(cannot)*
canvas *(sturdy cloth)*
  [canvass *(survey)*]
canyon
cap
  capped
  capping
capable
capacity
cape
capital *(1. money, 2. seat of government)*
  [capitol *(a statehouse)*]
captain
capture
  captured
  capturing
car
carat *(jeweler's measure)*
  [caret *(proofreader's mark)*]
  [carrot *(a vegetable)*]
carbon
  carbonation
card
cardboard
care
  caring
career
caret *(proofreader's mark)*

[carat *(jeweler's measure)*]
[carrot *(a vegetable)*]
carol *(a song)*
[carrel *(study space in a library)*]
cargo
  cargoes
carpet
carrel *(study space in a library)*
[carol *(a song)*]
carriage
carrot *(a vegetable)*
carat *(jeweler's measure)*]
[caret *(proofreader's mark)*]
carry
  carried
  carrier
  carries
cart
carve
  carved
  carver
  carving
case
  cased
  casing
cash *(money)*
[cache *(hiding place for goods)*]
  cashier
cast *(actors in a play)*
[caste *(social class)*]
castle
casual
cat
catch *(irreg. vb)*
  catches
caterpillar
cattle
Caucasian
caught
cause
  caused
  causing
caution
cave
  caved

caving

ce

cede *(give over; surrender)*
[seed *(part of a plant)*]
ceiling *(top of a room)*
[sealing *(closing)*]
celebrant
celebrate
  celebrated
  celebrating
  celebration
  celebrator
cell *(prison room)*
[sell *(exchange for money)*]
cellar *(basement)*
[seller *(one who sells)*]
cement
censor *(to ban)*
[sensor *(detection device)*]
cent *(penny)*
[sent *(did send)*]
[scent *(odor)*]
cents *(money)*
[sense *(feel)*]
center
central
century
  centuries
cereal *(food made from grain)*
[serial *(of a series)*]
ceremony
certain
  certainty
cession *(yielding)*
[session *(a meeting)*]

ch

chain
chair
chalk
challenge
  challenged
  challenger

challenging
chamber
champion
  championship
chance
  chanced
  chancing
change
  changed
  changing
  changeable
channel
chapter
character
  characteristic
  characteristically
charge
  charged
  charging
charm
chart
chase
  chased *(did chase)*
[chaste *(pure)*]
  chaser
  chasing
chat
  chatter
  chatty
cheap *(inexpensive)*
[cheep *(a bird sound)*]
cheat
check
cheek
cheep *(a bird sound)*
[cheap *(inexpensive)*]
cheer
cheese
chemical
cherry
  cherries
chest
chic *(stylish)*
[sheik *(Arab chief)*]

The following regular endings are not in the word list & can be added to the root word without changes: -s -ed -ing -er -est -ly -ful -less -ness. Most exceptions & root changes are in the list.

chicly
Chicago
  Chicagoan
chicken
chief
child
  children
Chile *(South American country)*
  [chilly *(cold)*]
  [chili *(hot pepper)*]
  Chilean
chimney
chin
China
  Chinese
chip
chocolate
choice
choir *(singing group)*
  [quire *(paper quantity)*]
choke
  choker
  choking
choose *(irreg. vb)*
  choosing
  choosey
chop
choral *(of a choir)*
  [coral *(sea-animal skeleton)*]
chorale *(sacred hymn)*
  [corral *(pen for livestock)*]
chord *(group of musical notes)*
  [cord *(string)*]
chorus
  choruses
chose
  chosen
Christ
  Christian
chromosome
chronological
chubby
chuckle
church
  churches
chute *(slide)*
  [shoot *(discharge gun)*]

ci

circle
  circled
  circling
circuit
circus
  circuses
cite *(give credit to a source)*
  [sight *(vision)*]
  [site *(location)*]
citizen
city
  cities
civil
  civilian
  civilization
  civilize
  civilized
  civilizing

cl

claim
  claimant
clam
clap
  clapped
  clapping
  clapper
clash
clasp
class
  classes
classify
  classification
  classifier
  classifies
classmate
classroom
clause *(part of a sentence)*
  [claws *(hooked nails on animals' feet)*]
claw
  claws *(hooked nails on animals' feet)*
  [clause *(part of a sentence)*]
clay
clean

clear
clerk
Cleveland
clever
click *(short, sharp sound)*
  [clique *(group of friends)*]
cliff
climate
climax
climb *(to ascend)*
  [clime *(climate)*]
cling
clip
clique *(group of friends)*
  [click *(short, sharp sound)*]
cloak
clock
  clocked
  clocking
close *(shut)*
  [clothes *(clothing)*]
  closed
  closes
  closing
close *(near)*
  closer
  closest
cloth
clothe
  clothed
  clothing
clothes *(clothing)*
  [close *(shut)*]
cloud
club
clue *(hint, helps solve a mystery)*
  [clew *(a ball of yarn)*]

co

coach
  coaches
coal *(fuel)*
  [cole *(food)*]
coarse *(rough)*
  [course *(1. path, 2. school subject)*]

coast
  coastal
coat
coax
  coaxes
code
  coded
  coder
  coding
coffee
coil
coin
cold
cole *(cabbage)*
  [coat *(fuel)*]
collage
collapse
  collapsed
  collapsing
collar
collect
  collector
  collection
college
  collegiate
collide
  collision
colonel *(military officer)*
  [kernel *(a seed or grain)*]
colony
  colonies
  colonial
  colonist
color
Colombia
Colorado
Columbus
column
coma *(state of consciousness)*
  [comma *(punctuation)*]
comb
combat
combine
  combined
  combining
  combination

come *(irreg. vb)*
  coming
comedy
  comedies
comet
comfort
comfortable
  comfortably
comic
  comical
comma *(punctuation)*
  [coma *(state of unconsciousness)*]
command
commence
  commenced
  commencing
commend
  commendable
  commendably
  commendation
comment
commerce
  commercial
  commercialism
commission
commit
  commitment
committee
common
commonplace
commotion
communicate
  communicated
  communicating
  communicator
  communication
Communist
Communism
community
  communities
compact
companion
company
  companies
compare
  compared
  comparing
  comparison
compass

compasses
compatible
compel
compensate
  compensated
  compensating
compete
competent
competition
complain
complement *(completing part)*
  [compliment *(praise)*]
complementary *(completes)*
  [complimentary *(free)*]
complete
  completed
  completing
complex
  complexes
  complexion
complicate
  complicated
  complication
compliment *(praise)*
  [complement *(completing part)*]
complimentary *(free)*
  [complementary *(completes)*]
component
compose
  composed
  composer
  composing
composite
  composition
compound
comprehend
  comprehension
compress
  compression
  compressor
compromise
compute
  computed

The following regular endings are not in the word list & can be added to the root word without changes: -s -ed -ing -er -est -ly -ful -less -ness. Most exceptions & root changes are in the list.

computing
computer
computation
comrade
concave
conceal
conceive
  conceived
concentrate
  concentrated
  concentrating
  concentration
concept
  conceptual
  conception
concern
concert
concession
conclude
  conclusion
concrete
condemn
  condemnation
condense
  condensed
condition
conduct
  conductor
cone
conference
confess
  confession
confide
  confident
  confidential
confine
  confined
  confining
confirm
conflict
conform
confront
  confrontation
confuse
  confused
  confusing
  confusion
congress
  congresses
  congressional
congruent
conjunction

connect
  connection
  connector
Connecticut
connotation
conquer
  conqueror
conscience *(noun)*
  [conscious *(adjective)*]
consecutive
consent
consequence
conserve
  conservation
consider
  considerable
  considerably
  considerate
consist
  consistence
  consistency
  consistent
consonant
constant
constitution
  constitutional
construct
  construction
consult
  consultation
consume
  consumed
  consumer
  consuming
  consumption
contact
contagious *(easily spread)*
  [contiguous *(near or close)*]
contain
content
contest
  contestant
continent
  continental
continue
  continued
  continuing
  continuous *(uninterrupted, unbroken)*

[continual *(no interruption, again and again)*]
continual *(no interruption, again and again)*
[continuous *(uninterrupted, unbroken)*]
continually
contract
contraction
contrary
contrast
contribute
  contributed
  contributing
  contributor
  contribution
control
  controllable
  controlled
  controller
  controlling
controversy
  controversial
convenient
  convenience
convention
  conventional
conversation
  conversational
converse
convert
  convertible
convex
convict
  conviction
convince
  convinced
  convincing
cook
cookie
cool
coop *(chicken pen)*
  [coupe *(type of car)*]
copper
copy
  copied
  copier
  copies
coral *(sea-animal skeleton)*

[choral *(of a choir)*]
cord *(string)*
[chord *(group of musical notes)*]
cordless
core *(the center)*
[corps *(group of military personnel)*]
cored
coring
corn
corps *(group of military personnel)*
[core *(the center)*]
corner
corral *(pen for livestock)*
[chorale *(sacred hymn)*]
correct
correction
correspond
correspondence
correspondent
corrupt
cosmic
cost *(irreg. vb)*
Costa Rica
costume
costumed
costuming
cottage
cotton
couch
cough
could
couldn't *(could not)*
council *(legislative body)*
[counsel *(to advise)*]
counsel *(to advise)*
[council *(legislative body)*]
counselor
count
country
countries
county
counties
coupe *(type of car)*

[coop *(chicken pen)*]
couple
coupled
coupling
courage
courageous
course *(1. path, 2. school subject)*
[coarse *(rough)*]
coursed
coursing
court
cousin
cover
cow
coward
cowboy

cr

crack
craft
crafty
crash
crashes
crawl
crayon
crazy
crazier
craziest
crazily
creak *(squeaking sound)*
[creek *(a stream)*]
cream
creamy
create
created
creating
creator
creation
creative
creature
credible
credit
creditor
credulous
creek *(a stream)*
[creak *(squeaking sound)*]

creep *(irreg. vb)*
crept
crew
crews *(groups of workers)*
[cruise *(an ocean voyage)*]
crib
crocodile
crop
cropped
cropping
cross
crow
crowd
crown
cruel
cruise *(an ocean voyage)*
[crews *(groups of workers)*]
crush
crushes
crust
cry
cried
crier
cries
crystal

cu

cub
Cuba
cube
cubed
cubing
cue *(to prompt)*
[queue *(line of people)*]
culture
cultural
cultured
culturist
cup
cupped
cupping
curious
curiosity
curl

The following regular endings are not in the word list & can be added to the root word without changes: -s -ed -ing -er -est -ly -ful -less -ness. Most exceptions & root changes are in the list.

current *(1. recent, 2. fast-flowing part of a stream)*
[currant *(small raisin)*]
curser *(one who curses)*
[cursor *(moving pointer on computer screen)*]
curtain
curvature
curve
  curved
  curving
cushion
custom
  customs
cut
  cutting

cy

cycle
  cycled
  cycling
  cyclist
cyclone
cylinder
  cylindrical
cymbal *(a percussion instrument)*
[symbol *(a sign)*]

cz

Czechoslovakia

da

dad
daily
dairy
  dairies
Dallas
dam *(stop flow)*
[damn *(curse)*]
  dammed
  damming
damage
  damaged
  damages
  damaging

damp
dance
  danced
  dancer
  dances
  dancing
danger
  dangerous
dare
  dared
  daring
dark
  darken
dash
date
  dated
  dating
datum
  data
daughter
dawn
day
  days *(parts of a week)*
  [daze *(to stun and confuse)*]
daylight
daze *(to stun and confuse)*
  [days *(parts of a week)*]

de

dead
deaf
deal
  dealt
dear *(much loved)*
  [deer *(type of animal)*]
death
decease
December
decide
  decided
  deciding
decimal
decision
deck
declare
  declared
  declaring

declaration
deep
  deepen
deer *(type of animal)*
  [dear *(much loved)*]
defeat
defect
defense
  defensible
  defensive
define
  defined
  defining
definite
  definition
degree
Delaware
delay
delicate
delicious
delight
delinquent
  delinquency
  delinquencies
deliver
  deliverance
  delivery
  deliveries
demand
Denmark
  Danish
denominator
dense
  denser
  density
  densities
Denver
deny
  denial
  denied
depart
department
depend
  dependable
  dependence
  dependency
  dependent
deposit
  depositor
depth
deputy
derive

derived
deriving
describe
  described
  describing
  description
desert *(leave)*
  [dessert *(pie)*]
  desertion
design
designate
  designated
  designating
  designation
desire
  desired
  desiring
  desirable
desk
despite
despot
dessert *(pie)*
  [desert *(leave)*]
destroy
destruction
detail
determine
  determined
  determining
Detroit
develop
  development
  developmental
device
devil
  deviltry
dew *(water)*
  [due *(owe)*]
  [do *(perform)*]

di

diagnosis
diagonal
diagram
  diagrammed
  diagramming
dial
diameter

diamond
dictionary
  dictionaries
did
didn't *(did not)*
die *(stop living)*
  [dye *(to color)*]
  died
  dying
diet
  dietitian
differ
  difference
  different
  differentiate
difficult
  difficulty
  difficulties
dig *(irreg. vb)*
  digger
  digging
digit
  digital
dim
  dimmed
  dimmer
  dimmest
dime
dimension
  dimensional
dine
  dined
  diner
  dining
dinner
dinosaur
dip
direct
  direction
  director
dirt
  dirty
  dirtier
  dirtiest
disable
disagree
  disagreement
  disagreeable
disappear

disappearance
disappoint
disapprove
disaster
disburse *(pay out)*
  [disperse *(scatter)*]
discomfort
discourage
discover
  discovery
  discoveries
discreet *(wisely cautious)*
  [discrete *(separate)*]
discrepancy
  discrepancies
discriminate
discuss
  discusses
  discussion
disease
disguise
dish
  dishes
disinterested *(impartial or without prejudice)*
  [uninterested *(indifferent or without interest)*]
dislike
disperse *(scatter)*
  [disburse *(pay out)*]
display
dispute
disrupt
dissolve
  dissolved
  dissolving
distant
  distance
distinguish
  distinguishable
  distinguishes
dive *(irreg. vb)*
  diver
  diving
diverge
  diverged

The following regular endings are not in the word list & can be added to the root word without changes: -s -ed -ing -er -est -ly -ful -less -ness. Most exceptions & root changes are in the list.

diverging
diverse
diversify
divide
divided
dividing
division
divisible
divisibility
divulge
divulged
divulging

do

do *(perform)* *(irreg. vb)*
[dew *(water droplets)*
[due *(payable)*]
dock
doctor
doe *(female deer)*
[dough *(bread mixture)*]
does
doesn't *(does not)*
dog
doll
dollar
done *(finished)*
[dun *(1. demand payment, 2. dull color)*]
donkey
don't *(do not)*
door
doorway
dot
dotted
dotting
double
doubled
doubling
doubt
dough *(bread mixture)*
[doe *(female deer)*]
dove
down
downed
downward
dozen

dr

drag
dragged
dragging
dragon
dramatic
dramatically
drank
draw *(irreg. vb)*
drawer
dream *(irreg. vb)*
dreamy
dress
dresses
drew
drift
drill
drilled
driller
drilling
drink *(irreg. vb)*
drive *(irreg. vb)*
driver
driving
drop
dropped
dropped
dropping
drove
drown
drug
drugged
drum
drummed
drummer
drumming
drunk
dry
dried
drier
dries
driest

du

dual *(two)*
[duel *(formal combat)*]
duck
ducked *(did duck)*
[duct *(tube or pipe)*]

due *(payable)*
[do *(perform)*]
[dew *(water droplets)*]
duel *(formal combat)*
[dual *(two)*]
dug
duke
dull
dully
dump
dumb
dun *(1. demand payment, 2. dull color)*
[done *(finished)*]
during
dust
Dutch
duty
duties

dy

dye *(color)*
[die *(stop living)*]
dyed

ea

each
eager
eagle
ear
early
earlier
earliest
earn *(work for)*
[urn *(vase)*]
earth
earthquake
ease
eased
easing
easily
east
eastern
easy
easier
easiest
eat *(irreg. vb)*

eb

ebb
ebony

ec

echo
  echoes
economy
  economies
  economic
Ecuador

ed

edge
  edged
  edger
  edging
educate
  education

ee

eerie
  eerier
  eerily
  eeriness

ef

effect *(noun)*
  [affect *(verb)*]
  effective
efficient
  efficiency
effort

eg

egg
Egypt
  Egyptian

ei

eight *(the number 8)*

ate *(did eat)*
eighth
eighteen
  eighteenth
eighty
  eighties
  eightieth
either

el

elect
  elector
  election
electric
  electrical
electrician
  electricity
electron
  electronic
element
elephant
elevate
  elevated
  elevating
  elevation
  elevator
eleven
  eleventh
else

em

emigrate *(leave your country)*
  [immigrate *(to come to a country to live)*]
  emigrated
  emigrating
  emigration
eminent *(famous, outstanding)*
  [imminent *(threaten to occur at any moment)*]
emotional
emperor
empire
employ

employable
empty
  emptied
  emptier
  empties
  emptiness

en

enable
  enabled
  enabling
enclose
  enclosure
encourage
  encouraged
  encouraging
encyclopedia
end
enemy
  enemies
energy
  energies
enforce
engage
  engaged
  engaging
engine
engineer
England
  English
enjoy
  enjoyable
enormous
enough
ensure *(make certain)*
  insure *(money)*
  ensured
  ensuring
enter
entertain
entire
entrance
entry
  entries
environment
  environmental

The following regular endings are not in the word list & can be added to the root word without changes: -s -ed -ing -er -est -ly -ful -less -ness. Most exceptions & root changes are in the list.

eq

equal
  equality
equation
equator
equip
  equipped
  equipping
equipment
equivalent

er

erase
  eraser
  erasing
error
  erroneous
erupt
  eruption

es

escape
  escaped
  escaping
Eskimo
especial
essential
establish
  establishes
estimate
  estimated
  estimating
  estimation
  estimator

eu

Europe
  European

ev

even
evening
event
eventual
ever
every

everybody
everyday
everyone
everything
everywhere
evidence
  evidenced
evil

ew

ewe *(female sheep)*
  [yew *(a shrub)*]
  [you *(yourself)*]

ex

exact
examination
examine
  examiner
  examined
  examining
example
except *(preposition)*
  [accept *(verb)*]
  exception
excerpt
exchange
  exchanged
  exchanging
excite
  excited
  exciting
  excitement
exclaim
exclude
excuse
  excused
  excusing
exercise
  exercised
  exercising
exert
  exertion
exhibit
  exhibitor
  exhibition
exhausted
  exhausting
  exhaustion
exist

existence
exit
expand
  expansion
expect
  expectation
expedition
expense
  expensive
experience
  experienced
  experiencing
experiment
  experimental
expert
explain
  explanation
explode
explore
  explored
  explorer
  exploring
  exploration
express
  expresses
  expression
extend
extra
extraordinary
extreme

ey

eye *(organ of sight)*
  [aye *(yes)*]
  [I *(myself)*]
  eyed
eyelet *(small hole)*
  [islet *(small island)*]

fa

fable
fabric
fabulous
face
  faced
  facing
fact

factory
  factories
factor
fail
faint *(weak)*
  [feint *(false attack)*]
fair *(1. honest, 2. a bazaar)*
  [fare *(cost of ticket)*]
fairy *(an imaginary being)*
  [ferry *(a river-crossing boat)*]
  fairies
faith
fall *(irreg. vb)*
fallen
fallible
false
familiar
family
  families
fan
  fanned
  fanning
fancy
  fancied
  fancier
  fancies
  fanciest
fantastic
far
fare *(cost of ticket)*
  [fair *(1. honest, 2. a bazaar)*]
farm
farther *(physical distance)*
  [further *(greater extent)*]
fascinate
  fascination
fashion
  fashionable
fast
fasten
fat
  fatter
  fattest

father
fault
favor
  favorable
  favorite
faze *(upset)*
  [phase *(a stage)*]

fe

fear
feast
feat *(accomplishment)*
  [feet *(plural of foot)*]
feather
feature
  featured
  featuring
February
fed
federal
feed *(irreg. vb)*
feel
feet *(plural of foot)*
  [feat *(accomplishment)*]
feint *(false attack)*
  [faint *(weak)*]
fell
fellow
felt
female
fence
  fenced
  fencing
ferry *(a river-crossing boat)*
  [fairy *(an imaginary being)*]
fertile
  fertility
festival
festive
fever
few

fi

fiber
field
fierce
  fiercer
  fiercest
fifteen
fifteenth
fifth
fifty
  fifties
  fiftieth
fig
fight
figure
  figured
  figuring
file
  filed
  filing
fill
film
final
find *(discover) (irreg. vb)*
  [fined *(forced to pay money as punishment)*]
fine
  fined *(forced to pay money as punishment)*
  [find *(discover)*]
  fining
  finer
  finest
finger
finish
  finishes
Finland
fir *(type of tree)*
  [fur *(animal covering)*]
fire
  fired
  firing

The following regular endings are not in the word list & can be added to the root word without changes: -s -ed -ing -er -est -ly -ful -less -ness. Most exceptions & root changes are in the list.

fireplace
firm
first
fish
　fishes
fisherman
　fishermen
fist
fit
　fitted
　fitting
five
　fifth
fix
　fixed
　fixes

fl

flag
　flagged
　flagging
flair *(natural talent)*
　[flare *(flaming signal)*]
flammable
　flammability
flame
　flamed
　flaming
flap
flare *(flaming signal)*
　[flair *(natural talent)*]
flash
　flashes
flat
　flatten
flaunt
flavor
flea *(insect)*
　[flee *(run away)*]
flee *(run away) (irreg. vb)*
　[flea *(insect)*]
fleet
flew *(did fly)*
　[flu *(influenza)*]
　[flue *(chimney part)*]
flight
flip
float

flood
floor
floral
Florida
flotation
flour *(milled grain)*
　[flower *(blossom)*]
flow
flower *(blossom)*
　[flour *(milled grain)*]
flu *(influenza)*
　[flew *(did fly)*]
　[flue *(chimney part)*]
flute
　fluted
　fluting
fly *(irreg. vb)*
　flies

fo

fog
　fogging
　foggy
fold
folk
follow
food
fool
foolish
foot
football
for *(in favor of)*
　[fore *(front part)*]
　[four *(the number 4)*]
forbade
forbid *(irreg. vb)*
force
　forced
　forcing
ford
fore *(front part)*
　[for *(in favor of)*]
　[four *(the number 4)*]
forehead
foreign
forest
forever
foreword *(a preface)*
　[forward *(toward the front)*]

forgave
forget
　forgettable
　forgetting
forgot
　forgotten
fork
form
formal
　formally *(adjective)*
　[formerly *(adverb)*]
formation
former
　formerly *(adverb)*
　[formally *(adjective)*]
formula
fort
forth *(forward)*
　[fourth *(after third)*]
fortune
　fortunate
forty
　forties
　fortieth
forward *(toward the front)*
　[foreword *(a preface)*]
fossil
fought
foul *(bad)*
　[fowl *(a bird)*]
found
four *(the number 4)*
　[for *(in favor of)*]
　[fore *(front part)*]
　fourth *(after third)*
　[forth *(forward)*]
fourteen
fourteenth
fowl *(a bird)*
　[foul *(bad)*]
fox
　foxes

fr

fraction
  fractional
frame
  framed
  framing
franc *(French money)*
  [frank *(honest)*]
France
frank *(honest)*
  [franc *(French money)*]
free
  freed
  freer
  freest
freedom
freeze *(irreg. vb)*
  freezing
French
frequent
  frequency
  frequencies
fresh
  freshen
friar *(member of religious order)*
  [fryer *(fryer chicken)*]
Friday
friend
  friendly
  friendlier
  friendliest
fright
frighten
frog
from
front
frontier
frost
froze
  frozen
fruit
fry
  fried
fryer *(frying chicken)*

[friar *(member of religious order)*]

fu

fuel
full
fun
function
funny
  funnier
  funniest
fur *(animal covering)*
  [fir *(type of tree)*]
furnace
furniture
further *(greater extent)*
  [farther *(physical distance)*]
future

ga

gain
gaiety
gallon
game
gang
garage
garden
garment
gas
  gases
gasoline
gate *(fence)*
  [gait *(pace)*]
gather
gauge
  gauged
  gauges
gave
gay

ge

gear
gene
general

generation
generous
genius
gentle
  gentled
  gentler
  gently
gentleman
  gentlemen
geography
  geographies
geology
geometry
  geometries
  geometric
  geometrically
Georgia
germ
German
  Germany
get *(irreg. vb)*
  getting

gh

ghastly
ghetto
ghost
ghoul

gi

giant
gift
gilt *(golden)*
  [guilt *(opposite of innocence)*]
girl
give *(irreg. vb)*
  giver
  giving

The following regular endings are not in the word list & can be added to the root word without changes: -s -ed -ing -er -est -ly -ful -less -ness. Most exceptions & root changes are in the list.

gl

glacial
glacier
glad
  gladder
  gladdest
glance
  glanced
  glancing
glass
  glasses
  glassy
glee
glimpse
glint
globe
  global
glory
  glories
  glorious
glow
glue
  glued
  gluing

gn

gnu *(antelope)*
  [knew *(did know)*]
  [new *(opposite of old)*]

go

go *(irreg. vb)*
  goes
goal
goat
god
gold
  golden
gone
good
good-bye
goose
gorilla *(type of ape)*
  [guerrilla *(irregular
  soldier)*]
got
government

governmental
governor

gr

grab
  grabbed
  grabbing
grace
grade
  graded
  grading
gradual
grain
grammar
grand
grandfather
grandmother
grant
grape
graph
grass
  grasses
grassland
grate *(to grind)*
  [great *(1. large, 2.
  excellent)*]
grave
gravity
  gravities
gray
graze
  grazed
  grazing
great *(1. large, 2.
  excellent)*
  [grate *(to grind)*]
Great Britain
Greece
  Greek
greed
green
greet
grew
grief
grieve
  grieved
  grieving
  grievance
grin
  grinned
  grinning

grind *(irreg. vb)*
grip
groan *(moan)*
  [grown *(mature;
  adult)*]
grocery
  groceries
ground
group
grow *(irreg. vb)*
  grown *(mature; adult)*
  [groan *(moan)*]
  growth

gu

guard
Guatemala
guerilla *(irregular
  soldier)*
  [gorilla *(type of ape)*]
guess
guest *(visitor)*
  [guessed
  (surmised)]
guide
  guided
  guiding
guidance
guilt *(opposite of
  innocence)*
  [gilt *(golden)*]
  guilty
guitar
  guitarist
gulf
gum
gun
  gunned
  gunner
  gunning
guy

ha

habit
  habitual
habitat
had
hadn't *(had not)*
hail *(frozen rain)*
  [hale *(healthy)*]
hair *(growth on head)*
  [hare *(type of rabbit)*]
Haiti
hale *(healthy)*
  [hail *(frozen rain)*]
half
halfway
hall *(passage between
  rooms)*
  [haul *(to carry)*]
halve *(to cut in half)*
  [have *(possess)*
hammer
hand
handicap
handle
  handled
  handling
handsome
  handsomer
  handsomest
handwriting
hang
hangar *(storage building)*
  [hanger *(tool for
  draping clothing)*]
happen
happy
  happier
  happiest
  happily
  happiness
harass
  harassment
harbor
hard
hardy
  hardier
  hardily
hare *(type of rabbit)*

[hair *(growth on head)*]
harm
harmony
  harmonious
harness
  harnesses
harsh
harvest
has
hat
  hatter
hatch
  hatches
hate
  hated
  hating
haul *(carry)*
  [hall *(passage
  between rooms)*]
have *(possess)*
  [halve *(cut in half)*]
  having
haven't *(have not)*
Hawaii
  Hawaiian
hawk
hay *(dried grass)*
  [hey *(expression to get
  someone's
  attention)*]

he

he
head
heal *(make well)*
  [heel *(back part of
  foot)*]
  [he'll *(he will)*]
health
  healthy
  healthier
  healthiest
  healthily
hear *(listen) (irreg. vb)*
  [here *(this place)*]
  heard *(listened)*
  [herd *(group of
  animals)*]

heart
heat
heaven
heavy
  heavier
  heaviest
  heavily
  heaviness
he'd *(he would)*
  [heed *(pay
  attention to)*]
heel *(back part of foot)*
  [heal *(make well)*]
  [he'll *(he will)*]
  heeled
height
heir *(successor)*
  [air *(what you
  breathe)*]
held
helicopter
he'll *(he will)*
  [heal *(make well)*]
  [heel *(back part of
  foot)*]
hello
helmet
help
hemisphere
hen
her
herd *(group of
  animals)*
  [heard *(listened)*]
here *(this place)*
  [hear *(listen)*]
hero
  heroes
  heroic
  heroine
herself
hew *(chop)*
  [hue *(a shade or color)*]

The following regular endings are not in the word list & can be added to the root word without changes: -s -ed -ing -er -est -ly -ful -less -ness. Most exceptions & root changes are in the list.

hey *(expression to get someone's attention)*
[hay *(dried grass)*]

hi

hi *(word of greeting)*
[high *(elevated)*]
hid
  hidden
hide *(irreg. vb)*
  hiding
high *(elevated)*
  [hi *(word of greeting)*]
highland
highway
hill
him *(that man or boy)*
  [hymn *(religious song)*]
himself
hip
hire *(employ)*
  [higher *(above)*]
his
Hispanic
history
  histories
hit
  hitter
  hitting

ho

hoard *(hidden supply)*
  [horde *(a crowd)*]
hoarse *(sounding rough and deep)*
  [horse *(type of animal)*]
hog
hold *(irreg. vb)*
hole *(an opening)*
  [whole *(complete)*]
  holey *(full of holes)*
  [holy *(sacred)*]
  [wholly *(completely)*]
home
  homey

homeward
homonym
Honduras
honest
  honesty
Honolulu
honor
  honorable
hook
hop
  hopped
  hopping
hope
  hoped
  hoping
horde *(a crowd)*
  [hoard *(hidden supply)*]
horizon
  horizontal
horn
horse *(type of animal)*
  [hoarse *(sounding rough and deep)*]
hospitable
  hospitality
hospital
  hospitalize
hostel *(inn for young travelers)*
  [hostile *(unfriendly)*]
hot
  hotter
  hottest
hotel
hour *(sixty-minute period)*
  [our *(belonging to us)*]
house
  housed
  housing
Houston
how
however
howl

hu

hue *(a shade or color)*
[hew *(chop)*]

huge
human
  humanism
  humanitarian
  humanity
  humanize
  humankind
  humanoid
humor
hump
hundred
hung
Hungary
hunger
hungry
  hungrier
  hungriest
  hungrily
hunt
hurry
  hurried
  hurriedly
hurt

hy

hydrogen
hymn *(religious song)*
  [him *(that man or boy)*]
hypocrite

i

I *(myself)*
  [aye *(yes)*]
  [eye *(organ of sight)*]

ic

ice
  iced
  icing
Iceland
icicle

id

I'd *(I would)*
Idaho
idea

ideal
  identify
  identifies
identity
  identities
idle *(lazy)*
  [idol *(object of worship)*]

if

if

ig

ignite
  ignited
  igniting
ignition
ignore
  ignorance
  ignorant

il

ill
I'll *(I will)*
  [aisle *(narrow path)*]
  [isle *(small island)*]
Illinois
illuminate
  illuminated
  illuminating
illustration

im

I'm *(I am)*
image
imagery
imagine
  imagined
  imagining
  imaginable
  imaginary
  imagination
immediate
  immediacy

immigrate *(to come to a country to live)*
  [emigrate *(leave your country)*]
immigrated
immigrating
immigrant
imminent
  (threaten to occur at any moment)
  [eminent *(famous, outstanding)*]
imply
  implied
  implies
important
  importance
impossible
  impossibly
  impossibility
impostor
impression
improve
  improved
  improving

in

in *(opposite of out)*
  [inn *(type of hotel)*]
inch
include
  included
  including
  inclusion
income
increase
  increased
  increasing
incredible
indeed
independent
  independence
index
India
  Indian
Indiana
Indianapolis

indicate
  indicated
  indicating
  indication
  indicative
individual
industry
  industries
  industrial
inert
  inertia
inevitable
  inevitability
  inevitably
infer
  inference
influence
  influenced
  influencing
  influential
influenza
information
  informative
initial
ink
inland
inn *(type of hotel)*
  [in *(opposite of out)*]
inner
innocent
insect
insert
inside
insist
  insistence
instance *(an example or a situation)*
  [instants *(very short periods of time)*]
instant
instead
instinct
instruct
  instruction
  instructive

The following regular endings are not in the word list & can be added to the root word without changes: -s -ed -ing -er -est -ly -ful -less -ness. Most exceptions & root changes are in the list.

instructor
instrument
  instrumentation
  instrumental
insure *(to issue or obtain
  insurance)*
  [ensure *(to secure,
  guarantee)*]
  insured
  insuring
  insurance
intend
intense *(extreme)*
  [intents *(purposes)*]
  intensify
  intensity
  intention
  intentional
  intensive
interest
interior
internal
international
interrupt
intersect
  intersected
  intersecting
  intersection
interval
interview
into
introduce
  introduced
  introducing
  introduction
invent
  inventor
  invention
investigate
  investigated
  investigating
  investigative
  investigator
  investigation
invisible
  invisibility
  invisibly
invite
  invited
  inviting
  invitation

involve
  involved
  involvement
  involving
invulnerable
Iowa

ir

Iran
Iraq
irate
Ireland
  Irish
iris
iron
irony
  ironic
  ironically

is

is *(irreg. vb)*
island
isle *(island)*
  [aisle *(narrow path)*]
  [I'll *(I will)*]
islet *(small island)*
  [eyelet *(small hole)*]
isn't *(is not)*
Israel
  Israeli
issue
  issued
  issuing

it

it
italic
it's *(it is)*
  [its *(belong to it)*]
Italy
  Italian
item
  itemize
itself

ja

jacket
Jacksonville
jail
  jailor
jam *(fruit jelly)*
  [jamb *(part of a door
  frame)*]
January
Japan
  Japanese
jar
  jarred
  jarring
jaw
jazz
  jazzy
  jazzier
  jazziest

je

jest
  jester
jet
  jetted
  jetting
jettison
jetty
  jetties
jewel

ji

jiggle
jigsaw
jingle
  jingled
  jingling
jinx
  jinxes

jo

job
jobholder
jobless
join
joint

joke
  joked
  joker
  joking
journal
journey
journeyman
joy

ju

judge
  judged
  judging
  judgment
juice
July
jump
June
jungle
junior
jury
just
justice
justify
  justifiable
  justification

ka

Kansas

ke

keep *(irreg. vb)*
kelp
Kentucky
kept
kernel *(a seed or grain)*
  [colonel
  *(military
  officer)*]
kettle
key
keynote
keypunch
keystone

ki

kick
kid
  kidded
  kidding
kill
kind
kindle
  kindled
  kindling
king
kingdom
kink
kitchen
kite
kitten

kn

knead *(mix with hands)*
  [need*(require)*]
knee
kneel *(irreg. vb)*
knew *(did know)*
  [gnu *(antelope)*]
  [new *(opposite of old)*]
knife
  knives
knight *(servant of a king)*
  [night*(evening)*]
knit *(weave with yarn)*
  [nit *(louse egg)*]
knock
knot *(tangle)*
  [not *(negative)*]
  knothole
knotty *(full of
  tangles)*
  [naughty *(bad)*]
  know *(familiar with)*
(irreg. vb)
  [no *(expression of
  refusal)*]
knowledge
  knowledgeable
  knowledgeably
known

ko

Korea

la

label
labor
laboratory
  laboratories
lack
lad
ladder
lady
  ladies
laid
lain *(past
  participle of lie)*
  [lane *(narrow street or
  path)*]
lake
lamb *(baby sheep)*
  [lam *(to leave
  quickly)*]
land
landscape
lane *(narrow street or
  path)*
  [lain *(past
  participle of lie)*]
language
lap
  lapped
  lapping
large
  larger
  largest
last
late
  later
  latest
Latin
latitude
  latitudinal

The following regular endings are not in the word list & can be added to the root word without changes: -s -ed -ing -er -est -ly -ful -less -ness. Most exceptions & root changes are in the list.

latter
laugh
  laughable
  laughter
law
lawn
lay *(past tense of lie)*
  (irreg. vb)
  [lei *(flower necklace)*]
layer
lazy
  lazier
  laziest
  lazily
  laziness

le

lead *(noun: a metal)*
  [led *(guided)*]
lead *(verb: to guide)*
  (irreg. vb)]
leaf
  leaves
league
leak *(to drip)*
  leek *(a vegetable)*
lean *(1. slender, 2. slant to the side)*
  [lien *(a legal aim)*]
leap *(irreg. vb)*
learn
lease
  leased *(rented)*
  [least *(smallest)*]
least *(smallest)*
  [leased *(rented)*]
leather
leave
  leaving
led *(guided)*
  [lead *(a metal)*]
leek *(a vegetable)*
  [leak *(to drip)*]
left
leg
legal
  legality
  legalize

legend
  legendary
leg
lei *(flower necklace)*
  [lay *(past tense of lie)*]
leisure
lend *(irreg. vb)*
length
lens
  lenses
less
lesser *(of less size)*
  [lessor *(one who rents property)*]
lesson *(instruction)*
[lessen *(make less)*]
lessor *(one who rents property)*
  [lesser *(of less size)*]
let
  letting
let's *(let us)*
letter
levee *(embankment)*
  [levy *(impose a tax)*]
level
lever
levy *(impose a tax)*
  [levee *(an embankment)*]

li

liable
liar
liberal
  liberalism
  liberalize
liberate
  liberation
Liberia
liberty
  liberties
library
  libraries
license
lichen *(fungus)*
  [liken *(compare)*]
lick
lid

lie *(1. falsify, 2. present tense of "to get in a prone position")* *(irreg. vb)*
  [lye *(alkaline solution)*]
  lying
lien *(a legal claim)*
  lean *(1. slender, 2. slant to the side)*
lieu *(instead of)*
  [Lou *(a name)*]
life
lifelike
lifeline
lifetime
lifework
lift
light *(irreg. vb)*
lightning
like
  liked
  liking
  liken *(compare)*
  [lichen *(fungus)*]
limb
limit
  limitation
line
  lined
  lining
link
  linkage
lion
lip
liquid
liquor
list
listen
literate
  literacy
literal
literature
little
  littler
  littlest
live

lived
living
lively
livelier
liveliest
liveliness
lizard

lo

load *(burden)*
  [lode *(vein of ore)*]
loaf
  loaves
loan *(something borrowed)*
  [lone *(single)*]
loathe
local
locate
  located
  locating
  location
lock
lode *(vein of ore)*
  [load *(burden)*]
log
  logged
  logger
  logging
logic
  logical
London
  Londoner
lone *(single)*
  [loan *(something borrowed)*]
  lonelier
  loneliest
long
longitude
look
loop
loose *(not fastened or restrained)*
  [lose *(to come to be without)*]
  looser
  loosest

loot *(steal)*
  [lute *(stringed musical instrument)*]
lord
Los Angeles
lose *(to come to be without) (irreg. vb)*
  [loose *(not fastened or restrained)*]
  loser
  losing
loss
  losses
lost
lot
Lou *(a name)*
  [lieu *(instead of)*]
Louisiana
loud
love
  loved
  lover
  loving
lovely
  lovelier
  loveliest
  loveliness
low
lowland

lu

luck
  luckless
lucky
  luckier
  luckiest
  luckily
lumber
lump
lunch
  lunches
lung
lute *(stringed musical instrument)*]
  [loot *(steal)*]
Luxembourg

ly

lye *(alkaline solution)*
  [lie *(falsify)*]

ma

Ma
machine
  machined
mad
  madder
  maddest
made *(manufactured)*
  [maid *(domestic servant)*]
magazine
magic
magnate *(person of power)*
  [magnet *(metal that attracts other metals)*]
magnet *(metal that attracts other metals)*
  [magnate *(person of power)*]
  magnetic
maid *(domestic servant)*
  [made *(manufactured)*]
mail *(sent by post)*
  [male *(man or boy)*]
main *(most important)*
  [Maine *(a state)*]
  [mane *(horse's neck hair)*]
Maine *(a state)*
  [main *(most important)*]
  mane *(horse's neck hair)*
maintain
  maintenance
maize *(Indian corn)*

The following regular endings are not in the word list & can be added to the root word without changes: -s -ed -ing -er -est -ly -ful -less -ness. Most exceptions & root changes are in the list.

[maze
*(confusing
network of paths)*]
major
  majority
  majorities
make
  maker
  making
male *(man or boy)*
  [mail *(send by post)*]
mall *(courtyard)*
  [maul *(mangle)*]
Mama
mammal
  mammalian
man
  manned
  manning
manage
  managed
  managing
  manageable
  management
  manager
mane *(horse's neck hair)*
  [main *(most
  important)*]
  [Maine *(a state)*]
manner *(way of
  behaving)*
  [manor *(mansion)*]
  mannered
mantel *(shelf over
  fireplace)*
  [mantle *(cloak)*]
manufacture
  manufactured
  manufacturing
  manufacturer
many
map
  mapped
  mapping
maple
marble
  marbled
March *(month)*
  [march *(to walk)*]
  marches
margin
  marginal
mark
market

marketable
marriage
  marriageable
marry
  married
Mars
marshal *(law officer)*
  [martial *(warlike)*]
mask
Maryland
mass
  massed *(grouped)*
  [mast *(tall, straight
  pole)*]
  masses
Massachusetts
mast *(tall, straight pole)*
  [massed *(grouped)*]
master
mat
match
  matches
mate
  mated
  mating
material
  materialism
  materialize
mathematical
matter
maul *(mangle)*
  [mall *(courtyard)*]
may *(requesting or
  granting of
  permission)*
  [May *(the month)*]
May *(the month)*
  [may *(requesting or
  granting
  permission)*]
maybe
mayor
maze *(confusing
  network of paths)*
  [maize *(Indian corn)*]

me

me
meadow
meal
mean *(irreg. vb)*
meander
meaning

meantime
meanwhile
measure
  measured
  measuring
  measurement
meat *(animal flesh)*
  [meet *(greet)*]
  [mete *(to deal out)*]
mechanic
  mechanical
medal *(an award)*
  [meddle *(interfere)*]
medicine
  medical
medieval
Mediterranean
medium
meek
meet *(greet)*
  [meat *(animal flesh)*]
  [mete *(to deal out)*]
  meeting
melody
  melodic
melt
member
memento
memoir
memories
  memories
  memorable
Memphis
men
mental
  mentality
mention
  mentionable
merchant
mercury
mercy
mere
merry
  merrier
  merriest
  merrily
  merriment
mess
  messy
message
  messenger
met

metal *(iron, gold, etc.)*
  [mettle *(courage)*]
  metallic
mete *(to deal out)*
  [meat *(animal flesh)*]
  [meet *(to greet)*]
meter
  metric
method
  methodical
  methodology
mettle *(courage)*
  [metal *(iron, gold, etc.)*]
Mexico
  Mexican

mi

mice
Michigan
microscope
  microscopic
middle
midnight
might *(1. may, 2. strength)*
  [mite *(small insect)*]
  mightier
  mightiest
  mighty
  mightily
mild
mile
mileage
military
milk
  milked
  milker
  milking
million
mill
  milled
  miller
  milling
Milwaukee
mind
mine
  mined
  miner *(coal digger)*

[minor *(a juvenile)*]
mining
mineral
mingle
  mingled
  mingling
miniature
minimum
  minimal
  minimize
ministry
Minnesota
minor *(a juvenile)*
  [miner *(coal digger)*]
minority
minus
minute
mirror
mischief
  mischievous
misconduct
misdemeanor
miserable
misery
misfortune
miss
  missed *(did not contact)*
  [mist *(fog)*]
  misses
  missing
Mississippi
Missouri
misspell
mist *(fog)*
  [missed *(did not contact)*]
mistake
  mistaken
  mistaking
  mistakable
  mistook
mister *(Mr.)*
mite *(small insect)*
  [might *(1. may, 2. strength)*]
mix
  mixes
  mixture

mo

moan *(groan)*
  [mown *(cut down)*]
mob
mobile
  mobility
mode *(the fashion)*
  [mowed *(cut down)*]
model
modem
modern
modify
  modifier
moist
  moisten
  moisture
mold
molecule
Mom
moment
  momentarily
  momentary
  momentous
  momentum
Monday
monetary
money
monkey
monotony
  monotonous
monster
  monstrosity
  monstrous
Montana
month
mood
  moody
  moodier
  moodiest
moon
  moonlike
  moonlight
  moonscape
moral *(concerned with right conduct)*

The following regular endings are not in the word list & can be added to the root word without changes: -s -ed -ing -er -est -ly -ful -less -ness. Most exceptions & root changes are in the list.

[morale *(state of mind regarding cheerfulness)*]
moralist
morality
more
moreover
morn *(morning)*
[mourn *(to grieve)*]
morning
mosquito
mosquitoes
moss
mosses
most
moth
mother
motion
motor
motorist
mount
mountain
mountaineer
mountainous
mountaintop
mourn *(to grieve)*
[morn *(morning)*]
mouse
mouth
move
moved
moving
movable
movement
movie
moviegoer
moviemaker
mow *(irreg. vb)*
mowed *(cut down)*
[mode *(the fashion)*]
mown *(cut down)*
[moan *(groan)*]

mu

much
mud
mug
mugger
mugging
mule
mull

multiple
multiply
multiplication
multitude
mumble
mummy
murder
murderer
murderous
murmur
muscle *(part of the body)*
[mussel *(shellfish)*]
museum
music
musical
musician
must
mustache
musty
mustier
mustiest
mustiness
mutual

my

my
myself
mystery
mysteries
mysterious
mysteriously
mystic
mystical
myth
mythical
mythology

na

nail
name
named
naming
narrow
nation
national
nationalism
nationalistic
nationality
native
natural
nature

naughty *(bad)*
[knotty *(full of tangles)*]
navy
navies
naval *(nautical)*
[navel *(depression in stomach)*]
nay *(no)*
[neigh *(horse's whinnying sound)*]

ne

near
nearby
neat
Nebraska
necessary
necessarily
necessity
neck
need *(require)*
[knead *(mix with hands)*]
needy
needle
needled
needling
negative
negativity
neigh *(horse's whinnying sound)*
[nay *(no)*]
Negro
neighbor
neighborhood
neighborly
neither
nerve
nervous
nest
net
netted
netting
Netherland
Netherlander
Nevada
never
nevertheless

new *(opposite of old)*
  [gnu *(antelope)*]
  [knew *(did know)*]
New Hampshire
New Jersey
New Mexico
New Orleans
New York
New Zealand
newspaper
next

ni

nice
  nicer
  nicest
niche
nickel
niece
night *(evening)*
  [knight *(servant of a king)*]
nine
  ninth
nineteen
  nineteenth
ninety
  nineties
  ninetieth
ninth
nit *(louse egg)*
  [knit *(weave with yarn)*]

no

no *(expression of refusal)*
  [know *(to be familiar with)*]
noble
  nobly
  nobility
nobody
  nobodies
nod
  nodded
  nodding
noise

noisy
  noisier
  noisiest
  noisily
none *(not any)*
  [nun *(Catholic sister)*]
nonsense
noon
  noonday
  noontime
nor
normal
  normally
  normality
North
north
  northern
North Carolina
North Dakota
northeast
  northeastern
northwest
  northwestern
Norway
  Norwegian
nose
  nosed
  nosing
nostalgia
  nostalgic
  nostalgically
not *(in no manner)*
  [knot *(tangle)*]
note
  notable
  notation
notebook
nothing
notice
  noticeable
notion
notorious
noun
nourish
  nourishment
November
now
nowhere

nu

nuclear
number
  numbered
  numbering
numeral
numerator
numerous
nun *(Catholic sister)*
  [none *(not any)*]
nurse
  nursed
  nursing
nut
nutrient
  nutrition
  nutritious

oa

oak
oar *(paddle for a boat)*
  [or *(word used to show choices)*]
  [ore *(mineral deposit)*]
oat

ob

obey
  obedient
  obedience
object
  objectify
  objection
  objective
obligate
  obligation
  obligatory
oblige
oblong
observe
  observable
  observant
  observation
  observatory
obtain
obvious

The following regular endings are not in the word list & can be added to the root word without changes: -s -ed -ing -er -est -ly -ful -less -ness. Most exceptions & root changes are in the list.

oc

occasion
occasionally
occupy
   occupied
   occupies
occur
   occurred
   occurring
   occurrence
ocean
o'clock *(of the clock)*
October

od

odd
ode *(a poem)*
   [owed *(did owe)*]
odor

of

of *(preposition)*
   [off *(adverb)*]
offal *(entrails)*
   [awful *(terrible)*]
offer
office
   officer
   official
offshore
often

oh

oh *(an exclamation)*
   [owe *(be indebted)*]
Ohio
oil
oilcan
oilcloth

ok

Oklahoma

ol

old
olive

olympiad
Olympic

om

omit
   omitted
   omitting

on

on
once
one *(the number 1)*
   [won *(triumphed)*]
ongoing
onion
only
onto
onshore
onstage
onward

op

open
opera
operate
   operation
   operational
   operator
opinion
   opinionated
opportune
   opportunity
   opportunities
   opportunist
oppose
   opposite
   opposition
oppress
oppression
   oppressive
option
   optional
   optionally

or

or *(word used to shows choices)*
   [oar *(paddle for a boat)*]

[ore *(mineral deposit)*]
Oregon
organism
organize
   organization
organ
origin
   original
   originality
   originate

ot

other
otherwise

ou

ought
ounce
our *(belonging to us)*
   [hour *(sixty-minute period)*]
ourselves
out
outdoors
outer
outline
   outlined
   outlining
outside

ov

oven
over
overall
overboard
overcoat
overcome
   overcame
   overcoming
overdo *(go to extremes)*
   [overdue *(a bill not paid on time)*]
overhead
overhear
overlap
overlay
overlook
overnight

overpower

overseas *(abroad)*
   [oversees
   (supervises)]

ow

owe *(be indebted)*
   [oh *(an
   exclamation)*]
owed *(did owe)*
   [ode *(poem)*]
owl
own

ox

ox
   oxen
oxygen
   oxygenate

oy
oyster

oz
ozone

pa
Pa
pace
Pacific
pack
   packed *(did pack)*
   [pact *(agreement)*]
package
pact *(agreement)*
   [packed *(did pack)*]
pad
paddle
page
paid
pail *(bucket)*
   [pale *(light in color)*]
pain
   [pane *(window glass)*]

pained
painstakingly
paint
pair *(two of a kind)*
   [pare *(to peel)*]
   [pear *(a fruit)*]
Pakistan
palace
palate *(roof of mouth)*
   [palette *(board that
   holds artist's pain)*]
   [pallet *(shovel-like
   tool)*]
pale *(light in color)*
   [pail *(bucket)*]
palette *(board that holds
   artist's paint)*
   [palate *(roof of
   mouth)*]
   pallet *(shovel-like
   tool)*]
palm
pan
Panama
pane *(window glass)*
   [pain *(discomfort)*]
pants
Papa
paper
parade
   paraded
   parading
paragraph
Paraguay
parallel
   parallelogram
pare *(to peel)*
   [pair *(two of a kind)*]
   [pear *(a fruit)*]
parent
parenthesis
   parentheses
   parenthetic
Paris
park
parody
   parodied
parrot
part
partial

participate
   participator
   participation
   participatory
participle
particle
particular
partition
partner
party
   parties
pass
   passed *(moved by)*
   [past *(former time)*]
passage
passageway
passenger
passerby
   passersby
past *(former time)*
   [passed *(moved by)*]
paste
pasture
pat
patch
   patches
path
patience *(ability to
   endure)*
   [patients *(sick
   persons)*]
patient
   patients *(sick
   persons)*
   [patience *(ability to
   endure)*]
pattern
pause *(brief stop)*
   [paws *(feet of
   animals)*]
paw
   paws *(feet of
   animals)*
   [pause *(brief stop)*]
pay *(irreg. vb)*

pe
peace *(tranquility)*
   [piece *(part of a
   whole)*]

*The following regular endings are not in the word list & can be added to the root word without
changes: -s -ed -ing -er -est -ly -ful -less -ness. Most exceptions & root changes are in the list.*

peach
  peaches
peak *(mountaintop)*
  [peek *(sneak a look)*]
  [pique *(spark interest)*]
peal *(ringing sound)*
  [peel *(skin or rind of fruit)*]
peanut
pear *(a fruit)*
  pair *(two of a kind)*]
  [pare *(to peel)*]
pearl *(jewel)*
  [purl *(knitting stitch)*]
peculiar
pedal *(ride a bike)*
  [peddle *(sell)*]
peddle *(sell)*
  [pedal *(ride a bike)*]
peek *(sneak a look)*
  [peak *(mountaintop)*]
  [pique *(spark interest)*]
peel *(skin or rind of fruit)*
  [peal *(ringing sound)*]
peer *(an equal)*
  [pier *(a dock)*]
pen
pencil
peninsula
Pennsylvania
penny
  pennies
people
  peopled
pepper
per *(for each)*
  [purr *(cat sound)*]
percent
  percentage
perfect
perform
  performance
perhaps
perimeter
period
  periodical
permanent
  permanence
permit

permitted
permitting
perpendicular
persecute
persevere
  persevered
  persevering
  perseverance
person
personal *(of one person)*
  [personnel *(employees of a company)*]
personality
  personalities
personnel *(employees)*
  [personal *(of one person)*]
persuade
  persuaded
  persuading
Peru
pet
  petted
  petting

ph

phase *(a stage)*
  [faze *(upset)*]
Philadelphia
  Philadelphian
Philippines
Phoenix
photograph
  photographic
  photography
phrase
  phrased
  phrasing
physical
physician

pi

pi *(a Greek letter)*
  [pie *(type of pastry)*]
piano
  pianist
pick
  picked

picking
picnic
  picnicked
  picnicker
  picnicking
picture
  pictured
  picturing
pie *(kind of pastry)*
  [pi *(a letter in the Greek alphabet)*]
piece *(part of a whole)*
  [peace *(tranquility)*]
  pieced
  piecing
pier *(a dock)*
  [peer *(an equal)*]
pig
pigeon
pile
  piled
  piling
pilgrim
  pilgrimage
pilot
pin
  pinned
  pinning
pinch
pink
pioneer
pipe
  piped
  piping
pique *(spark interest)*
  [peak *(mountaintop)*]
  [peek *(sneak a look)*]
pirate
  pirated
  pirating
  piracy
pit
pitch
pity
  pitied
  pities
  pitiable
  pitiably
  pitiful
  pitiless

pl

place
  placed
  placing
plain *(not fancy)*
  [plane *(flat surface)*]
plaintive
plait *(braid)*
  [plate *(dish)*]
plan
  planned
  planner
  planning
plane *(flat surface)*
  [plain *(not fancy)*]
  planed
  planing
planet
  planetarium
  planetary
plant
plastic
  plasticity
plate *(dish)*
  [plait *(braid)*]
  plated
  plating
plateau
  plateaus or
  plateaux
platform
platitude
Plato
  platonic
platoon
play
playground
playmate
playwright
plaza
pleasant
please *(to make glad)*
  [pleas *(appeals)*]
pleasure
  pleasurable
plenty
  plentiful
plot

plotted
plotting
plow
plug
plum *(a fruit)*
  [plumb *(a lead weight)*]
plunder
plural
plus

po

pocket
poem
poet
  poetic
  poetry
poignant
point
  pointy
poise
  poised
poison
  poisonous
Poland
polar
pole *(a stick)*
  [poll *(an election)*]
  poled
  poling
police
  policed
  policing
policeman
  policemen
policewoman
policewomen
policy
  policies
polish
polite
politics
  political
poll *(an election)*
  [pole *(a stick)*]
pollen
polyester
polygraph
pond

ponder
ponderous
pony
  ponies
pool
poor
pop
  popped
  popping
popular
  popularity
population
porch
pore *(tiny opening in skin)*
  [pour *(to make liquid flow)*]
port
portion
portrait
portray
Portugal
pose
  posed
  poser
  posing
position
positive
possess
  possession
  possessive
possible
  possibly
  possibility
  possibilities
post
pot
  potted
  potter
  potting
potato
  potatoes
potent
potential
pottery
pound
pour *(to make liquid flow)*
  [pore *(tiny opening in skin)*]
powder
power

The following regular endings are not in the word list & can be added to the root word without changes: -s -ed -ing -er -est -ly -ful -less -ness. Most exceptions & root changes are in the list.

pr

practical
practice
  practiced
  practicing
prairie
praise
  praised
  praising
praiseworthy
  praiseworthiness
pray *(worship)*
  [prey *(animal hunted for food)*]
  prayer
precede
  preceded
  preceding
precious
precise
predicate
  predicated
prefer
  preferred
  preferring
  preference
  preferential
prefix
  prefixes
prepare
  prepared
  preparing
preparation
preposition
  prepositional
presence
present *(1. make a gift to, 2. stage a play or show)*
present *(1. the time now, 2. being in attendance)*]
president
  presidential
press
pressure
  pressured
  pressuring
presume
  presumed
  presuming
  presumption

pretend
  pretense
  prestension
  pretentious
pretty
  prettied
  prettier
  pretties
  prettiest
  prettily
  prettiness
prevail
  prevalent
  prevalence
prevent
  prevention
previous
prey *(animal hunted for food)*
  [pray *(worship)*]
price
  priced
  pricing
prickly
  pricklier
  prickliest
  prickliness
pride *(self-esteem)*
  [pried *(1. inquired in a nosey way, 2. move with a lever)*]
  prided
  priding
priest
  priestess
prim
primal
primary
  primaries
  primarily
primate
prime
  primed
  priming
primitive
prince
princess
  princesses
principal *(1. most important, 2. head of school)*
  [principle *(fundamental law)*]
print

prior
priority
  priorities
prison
pristine
private
privilege
  privileged
prize
probable
  probably
  probability
  probabilities
problem
  problematic
proceed
  procedure
process
prodigious
produce
  produced
  producer
  producing
product
  production
  productive
  productivity
profession
  professional
  professor
profit *(gain in money)*
  [prophet *(seer; visionary)*]
profound
program
  programmed
  programmer
  programming
progress *(1. gradual betterment, 2. to move forward)*
prohibit
  prohibitive
project
promise
  promised
  promising
promote
  promoted
  promoter
  promoting
pronoun
pronounce

pronounced
pronouncing
pronunciation
proofread
propaganda
  propagandist
  propagandize
  propagandized
  propagandizing
propel
  propelled
  propelling
  propeller
proper
property
  properties
prophet *(seer; visionary)*
  [profit *(gain in money)*]
proportion
propose
  proposal
proposition
prose
prosecute
  prosecuted
  prosecuting
  prosecutor
  prosecution
prosper
  prosperity
  prosperous
protect
  protection
  protective
protein
proud
prove
  proved
  proven
  proving
provide
  provided
  providing
province
pry
  pried *(1. inquired in a nosey way, 2. moved with a lever)*

[pride *(self-esteem)*]

ps

pseudonym
psychiatry
  psychiatric
  psychiatrist
psychology
  psychologist

pu

public
publicity
  publicist
publish
  publication
pull
pump
punctuate
punish
  punishment
pupil
puppy
  puppies
purchase
  purchased
  purchaser
  purchasing
pure
  purer
  purest
  purity
purl *(knitting stitch)*
  [pearl *(jewel)*]
purple
  purplish
purpose
purr *(cat sound)*
  [per *(for each)*]
pursue
  pursued
  pursuing
push
  pushes
put *(irreg. vb)*
  putting
puzzle

puzzled
puzzling

py

pyramid
pyre
python

qu

qualify
  qualified
  qualifies
quality
  qualities
quantity
  quantities
  quantify
quart
quarter
quarterback
quartet
quarts *(measure)*
  [quartz *(mineral)*]
queasy
  queasier
  queasiest
  queasiness
queen
queer
quench
  quenches
question
queue *(line of people)*
  [cue *(to prompt)*]
quick
  quicken
quiet *(adjective)*
  [quite *(adverb)*]
quit
quite *(adverb)*
  [quiet *(adjective)*]
quiver
quiz
  quizzed
  quizzes
  quizzing
quizzical
  quizzically

The following regular endings are not in the word list & can be added to the root word without changes: -s -ed -ing -er -est -ly -ful -less -ness. Most exceptions & root changes are in the list.

quota
quote
  quoted
  quoting
  quotable
  quotation
quotient

ra

rabbi
rabbit
raccoon
race
  raced
  racer
  racing
radiation
radical
  radicalism
radio
radioactive
  radioactivity
radius
raft
rag
rage
  raged
  raging
rail
railroad
rain *(precipitation)*
  [reign *(royal rule)*]
  [rein *(harness)*]
  rainy
  rainier
  rainiest
rainfall
raise *(put up)*
  [raze *(tear down)*]
  [rays *(beams of energy)*]
  raised
  raising
rampant
  rampantly
ran *(irreg. vb)*
ranch
  rancher
  ranches
  ranching
rang
range

ranged
ranger
ranging
rank
  ranked
  ranking
rap *(hit)*
  [wrap *(cover)*]
  rapped
  rapping
rapid
  rapidity
rare
  rarely
  rarer
  rarest
  rarity
rat
rate
  rated
  rater
  rating
rather
ratio
ration
  rational
  rationally
  rationalism
  rationalize
rationale
rat
raw
ray
  rays *(beams of energy)*
  [raise *(put up)*]
  [raze *(tear down)*]

re

reach
  reaches
reaction
  reactionary
reactor
read *(scan printed matter)* *(irreg. vb)*
  [reed *(a plant)*]
  reader
  reading
read *(1. past tense of verb, 2. scanned printed matter)*
  [red *(a color)*]

ready
  readied
  readying
real *(genuine)*
  [reel *(spool)*]
  really
  realism
  reality
  realities
realize
  realized
  realizing
  realization
rear
  reared
  rearing
reason
  reasonable
  reasonably
rebel
  rebelled
  rebelling
  rebellion
  rebellious
recall
receipt
receive
  received
  receiver
  receiving
recent
receptacle
reception
  receptionist
receptive
recipe
recipient
reciprocal
reciprocate
  reciprocated
  reciprocating
recognize
  recognized
  recognizing
  recognizance
  recognition
recollect
  recollection
recommend
  recommendation
recompense
  recompensed

recompensing
reconcile
  reconciled
  reconciling
  reconciliation
record
recover
rectangle
  rectangular
rectify
  rectified
  rectifies
  rectifying
red (a color)
  [read (scanned printed matter)]
  redder
  reddest
  redness
reduce
  reduced
  reducing
reed (a plant)
  [read (scan printed matter)]
reek (give off strong odor)
  [wreak (inflict)]
reel (spool)
  [real (genuine)]
refer
  referred
  referring
reference
referendum
  referenda
reflect
  reflector
  reflection
refrigerate
  refrigeration
  refrigerator
refuse
  refused
  refusing
regard
region
  regional
  regionalism
regret
  regrettable
  regretted

regretting
regular
reign (royal rule)
  [rain (precipitation)]
  [rein (harness)]
relate
  related
  relating
relation
  relationship
relative
  relativism
  relativity
relax
  relaxation
release
  released
  releasing
relief
  relieve
  relieved
  relieving
religion
  religiosity
  religious
remain
  remainder
remarkable
  remarkably
remember
  remembrance
remind
reminisce
  reminiscent
  reminiscence
  reminiscing
remiss
  remission
remit
  remitted
  remitter
  remitting
remorse
remote
  remotest
  remoter
remove
  removed
  remover

removing
removable
rename
rendezvous
renounce
  renounced
  renouncing
  renunciation
rent
reorganize
  reorganized
  reorganizer
  reorganizing
  reorganization
repair
repeal
repeat
  repetition
  repetitious
repel
  repelled
  repelling
  repellent
repent
  repentant
  repentance
repercussion
repertoire
  repertory
repetition
  repetitious
replace
  replaceable
  replaced
  replacing
  replacement
replicate
  replicated
  replicating
  replication
reply
  replied
report
represent
  representation
  representative
reprieve
  reprieved
  reprieving
reproach

The following regular endings are not in the word list & can be added to the root word without changes: -s -ed -ing -er -est -ly -ful -less -ness. Most exceptions & root changes are in the list.

reptile
  reptilian
republic
  Republican
repudiate
  repudiated
  repudiating
  repudiation
repulse
  repulsed
  repulsing
  repulsion
reputation
repute
require
  required
  requiring
requirement
requisite
  requisition
rescue
  rescued
  rescuer
  rescuing
research
resemble
  resemblance
  resembled
  resembling
resist
  resistance
  resistant
resolute
  resolution
resolve
  resolved
  resolving
resonant
  resonance
resource
respect
  respectably
  respectability
respectfully *(showing
politeness)*
  [respectively *(in
regard to each of a
number in the order
given)*]
respective
  respectively
  *(in regard to each of a
number in the order
given)*

[respectfully
*(showing
politeness)*]
respond
responsible
  responsibility
  responsibilities
responsive
rest *(relax)*
  [wrest *(take from)*]
restaurant
  restaurateur
restless
result
  resultant
resume *(take up again)*
  resumed
  resuming
  resumption
resume *(short
account of one's career)*
resurrect
  resurrection
retain
retaliate
retention
  rententive
reticent
  reticence
retinue
retire
retort
return
  returnable
reveal
review
revelation
Reverend
revolution
  revolutionary
revolt
reward
rewrite
  rewrote
  rewriting
  rewritten

rh

Rhine River
rhinocerous
Rhode Island

rhyme *(repetition of same
sounds)*
  [rime *(type of ice;
frost)*]
rhymed
rhymer
rhyming
rhythm
rhythmic
rhythmical

ri

rib
  ribbed
  ribbing
ribbon
rice
rich
  riches
ride *(irreg. vb)*
  rider
  riding
ridge
ridicule
  ridiculous
rifle
  rifled
  rifling
right *(correct)*
  [rite *(ceremony)*]
  [write *(inscribe)*]
rigid
rime *(type of ice; frost)*
  [rhyme *(repetition of
same sounds)*]
ring *(circular band)*
  [wring *(squeeze)*]
ring *(irreg. vb)*
rink
riot
rip
  ripped
  ripping
ripe
  ripen
rise *(irreg. vb)*
  rising
risk
  risky
rite *(ceremony)*
  [right *(correct)*]
  [write *(inscribe)*]

rival
  rivalry
  rivalries
river

ro

road *(street)*
  [rode *(traveled)*]
  [rowed *(used oars)*]
roar
robot
  robotic
rock
  rocky
rocket
rode *(traveled)*
  [road *(street)*]
  [rowed *(used oars)*]
roe *(fish eggs)*
  [row *(1. a line. 2. use oars)*]
role *(a part played)*
  [roll *(1. turn over, 2. bread)*]
roll *(1. turn over, 2. bread)*
  [role *(a part played)*]
Rome
  Roman
romance
  romanced
  romancing
  romantic
  romantically
root *(part of a plant)*
  [route *(roadway)*]
  rooted
  rooter
  rooting
rope
  roped
  roper
  roping
rose *(type of flower)*
  [rows *(1. lines; 2. uses oars)*]
rote *(by memory)*
  [wrote *(did write)*]

rough *(not smooth)*
  [ruff *(pleated collar)*]
round
route *(roadway)*
  [root *(part of a plant)*]
  routed
  routing
row *(1. a line, 2. use oars)*
  [roe *(fish eggs)*]
  rowed *(used oars)*
  [road *(street)*]
  [rode *(traveled)*]
royal

ru

rub
  rubbed
  rubbing
rubber
  rubbery
ruby
rude *(impolite)*
  [rued *(regretted)*]
rues *(regret)*
  [ruse *(subterfuge)*]
rug
  rugged
rule
  ruled
  ruler
  ruling
Rumania
rumor
run *(irreg. vb)*
  runner
  running
runaway
rung *(a step on a ladder)*
  [wrung *(squeezed)*]
ruse *(subterfuge)*
  [rues *(regret)*]
rush
  rushes
Russia
  Russian
rust
rusty

ry

rye *(grain)*
  [wry *(ironically humorous)*]

sa

sack
sacrifice
sad
  sadden
  sadder
  saddest
saddle
  saddled
  saddling
safe
  safer
  safest
safety
  safeties
said
sail *(travel by boat)*
  [sale *(selling at bargain prices)*]
  sailor
saint
salad
sale
salmon
salt
  salty
  saltier
  saltiest
salute
  saluted
  saluting
Salvador
same
sample
  sampled
  sampler
  sampling
San Antonio
San Diego
San Francisco
San Jose
sand
  sandy

The following regular endings are not in the word list & can be added to the root word without changes: -s -ed -ing -er -est -ly -ful -less -ness. Most exceptions & root changes are in the list.

sandal
sandwich
  sandwiches
sang
sank
Santa Claus
sap
sash
sat
satellite
satin
satisfy
  satisfied
  satisfaction
  satisfactory
Saturday
sauce
  saucer
  saucy
save
  saved
  saver
  saving
saw *(irreg. vb)*
say *(irreg. vb)*

sc

scale
  scaled
  scaling
scar
scarce
  scarcer
  scarcest
scarcity
scare
  scared
  scaring
  scary
  scarier
  scariest
scarf
  scarves
scatter
scene *(setting)*
  [seen *(viewed)*]
scent *(smell)*
  [sent *(did send)*]
  [cent *(penny)*]
schedule
  scheduled
  scheduling

scholar
scholarly
scholarship
school
science
scientific
  scientifically
scientist
scissor
scold
scoop
scoot
  scooter
scope
scorch
score
  scored
  scorer
  scores
  scoring
scout
scraggly
scramble
  scrambled
  scrambling
scrap
  scrapped
  scrapping
scratch
  scratches
  scratchy
scrawl
scrawny
  scrawnier
  scrawniest
scream
screech
screen
screenplay
screenwriter
screw
screwdriver
scribble
  scribbled
  scribbler
  scribbling
scrimp
script
scroll
scrub
  scrubbed
  scrubbing
  scrubby

scrubbier
scrubbiest
scruff
scuff
  scuffed
  scuffing
scull *(racing boat)*
  [skull *(the head)*]
sculptor
sculpture
  sculptured
  sculpturing
scum
  scummed
  scumming
scurry

se

sea *(ocean)*
  [see *(visualize)*]
seal
sealing *(closing)*
  [ceiling *(top of room)*]
seam *(where two pieces meet)*
  [seem *(give the impression of being)*]
seamy
sear *(singe)*
  [seer *(prophet; visionary)*]
search
  searches
season
  seasonable
  seasonal
seat
Seattle
seaward
second
  secondary
secrecy
secret
  secretive
secretary
  secretarial
  secretaries
section
  sectional
secure
  secured

securing
security
  securities
sedate
  sedated
  sedating
  sedative
see *(visualize)*
  (irreg. vb)
  [sea *(ocean)*]
seed *(part of a plant)*
  [cede *(give over; surrender)*]
seek *(irreg. vb)*
seem *(give the impression of being)*
  [seam *(where two pieces join)*]
seen *(viewed)*
  [scene *(setting)*]
seer *(prophet; visionary)*
  [sear *(singe)*]
segment
seize
  seized
  seizes
  seizing
  seizure
seldom
select
  selection
  selective
self
sell *(exchange for money) (irreg. vb)*
  [cell *(prison room)*]
  seller *(one who sells)*
  [cellar *(basement)*]
semester
senate
  senator
send *(irreg. vb)*
  sent *(did send)*
  [cent *(penny)*]
  [scent *(odor)*]
senior
  seniority
sense *(feel)*
  [cents *(pennies)*]
  sensed

senseless
sensing
sensible
  sensibly
  sensibility
sensitive
sensor *(detection device)*
  [censor *(ban)*]
  sensory
sent *(did send)*
  [cent *(penny)*]
  [scent *(smell)*]
sentence
  sentenced
  sentencing
separate
  separated
  separating
  separation
September
serf *(feudal servant)*
  [surf *(ocean waves)*]
sergeant
series
serial *(of a series)*
  [cereal *(food made from grain)*]
serious
serpent
  serpentine
servant
serve
  served
  server
  serving
service
  serviced
  servicing
session *(a meeting)*
  [cession *(yielding)*]
set
setting
settle
  settled
  settles
  settling
  settlement
  settler
seven

seventh
seventeen
seventeenth
seventy
  seventies
  seventieth
several
severe
  severity
sew *(mend) (irreg. vb)*
  [so *(in order that)*]
  [sow *(plant seeds)*]
sewage
sewer
sewn

sh

shabby
  shabbier
  shabbiest
  shabbily
  shabbiness
shackle
  shackled
  shackling
shade
  shaded
  shading
  shadier
  shadiest
  shady
shadow
  shadowy
shaft
shake *(irreg. vb)*
  shaker
  shakier
  shakiest
  shaking
  shaky
shaken
shall
shallow
shamble *(walk awkwardly or unsteadily)*
  shambled
  shambling

The following regular endings are not in the word list & can be added to the root word without changes: -s -ed -ing -er -est -ly -ful -less -ness. Most exceptions & root changes are in the list.

shambles *(confusion; a mess)*
shame
  shamed
  shaming
shamefaced
shampoo
shape
  shaped
  shapeliest
  shaping
share
  shared
  sharer
  sharing
shark
sharp
shave
  shaved
  shaven
  shaver
  shaving
shear *(cut)*
  [sheer *(transparent)*]
shed
  shedding
she
she'd *(she had, she would)*
sheep
sheer *(transparent)*
  [shear *(cut)*]
sheet
sheik *(Arab chief)*
  [chic *(stylish)*]
shelf
  shelves
  shelved
  shelving
shell
she'll *(she will)*
shelter
shepherd
sheriff
she's *(she has, she is)*
shield
shift
  shifty
  shiftier
  shiftiest
  shiftiness
shine *(irreg. vb)*

shining
shiny
shinier
shiniest
ship
  shipped
  shipping
shirt
shock
shoe *(foot covering)*
  [shoo *(chase away)*]
shone *(beamed)*
  [shown *(exhibited)*]
shoo *(chase away)*
  [shoe *(foot covering)*]
shook *(irreg. vb)*
shoot *(discharge gun)*
  [chute *(slide)*]
shop
  shopped
  shopper
  shopping
shore
  shored
  shoring
short
shot
shotgun
should
shoulder
shout
shovel
show *(irreg. vb)*
shower
shown *(exhibited)*
  [shone *(beamed)*]
showcase
  showcased
  showcasing
showroom
shrank
shred
shriek
shrill
shrink *(irreg. vb)*
  shrinkage
shrug
  shrugged
  shrugging
shrunk
shuffle
  shuffled

shuffling
shut *(irreg. vb)*
  shutting
shy
  shier
  shiest

si

Siam
sick
  sicken
  sickening
side *(flank)*
  [sighed *(breathed audibly)*]
  sided
  siding
sidewalk
sideways
sigh
  sighed *(breathed audibly)*
  [side *(flank)*]
  sighing
  sighs *(audible breaths)*
  [size *(physical dimension)*]
sight *(vision)*
  [cite *(give credit to a source)*]
  [site *(location)*]
  sighted
  sighting
sign *(signal)*
  [sine *(trigonometric function)*]
signal
signature
significant
  significance
silent
  silence
  silenced
  silencer
  silencing
silk
  silken
  silky
silly
  sillier
  silliest

silliness
silver
 silvery
similar
 similarity
 similarities
simile
simmer
simper
simple
 simpler
 simplest
simply
 simplicity
simplify
 simplified
 simplifies
 simplifying
simulate
 simulated
 simulating
 simulation
simultaneous
since
sine *(trigonometric function)*
 [sign *(signal)*]
sing *(irreg. vb)*
single
 singled
 singling
singular
 singularity
 singularities
sink *(irreg. vb)*
sip
 sipped
 sipping
sir
sister
sit *(irreg. vb)*
 sitter
 sitting
site *(location)*
 [cite *(give credit to a source)*]
 [sight *(vision)*]
situate
 situated
 situating

situation
situational
six
 sixes
 sixth
sixteen
 sixteenth
sixty
 sixties
 sixtieth
size *(physical dimension)*
 [sighs *(audible breaths)*]
 sized
 sizing

sk

skate
skeleton
 skeletal
skeptic
 skeptical
 skepticism
sketch
ski
 skied
 skiing
skid
 skidded
 skidding
skill
skin
skip
 skipped
 skipper
 skipping
skirt
skull *(head)*
 [scull *(racing boat)*]
skunk
sky
 skies

sl

slack
 slacken
slam

slammed
 slamming
slang
slant
slap
 slapped
 slapping
slave
 slaved
 slaving
 slavery
slay *(kill)*
 [sleigh *(sled)*]
sled
 sledded
 sledding
sleep *(irreg. vb)*
 sleepy
 sleepier
 sleepiest
 sleepily
 sleepiness
sleeve
sleigh *(sled)*
 [slay *(kill)*]
sleight *(skill)*
 [slight *(slender)*]
slept
slice
 sliced
 slicing
slid
slide *(irreg. vb)*
 slider
 sliding
slight *(slender)*
 sleight *(skill)*
slim
 slimmer
 slimmest
 slimming
slip
 slipped
 slipping
 slippery
slope
 sloped
 sloping
sloppy
 sloppier

The following regular endings are not in the word list & can be added to the root word without changes: -s -ed -ing -er -est -ly -ful -less -ness. Most exceptions & root changes are in the list.

sloppiest
slot
  slotted
  slotting
slow
slug
  slugged
  slugging
  sluggish
slumber
slump

sm
small
smart
  smarten
smash
smear
smell
  smelly
  smellier
  smelliest
smile
  smiled
  smiling
smoke
  smoked
  smoker
  smoking
  smoky
smooth
smother

sn
snack
snag
  snagged
  snagging
snake
  snaked
  snaking
snap
  snapped
  snapping
  snappy
sneak
sneeze
sniff
snip
  snipped
  snipping

snippy
snore
  snored
  snoring
snow
  snowy
snowball
snowfall
snowflake
snowman
snowstorm
snub
  snubbed
  snubbing
snuggle

so
so *(in order that)*
  [sew *(mend)*]
  [sow *(plant seeds)*]
soak
soap
  soapy
soar *(fly)*
  [sore *(painful)*]
social
society
  societies
sock
soda
sofa
soft
soil
sold *(did sell)*
  [soled *(bottom placed on a shoe)*]
sole
solicit
  solicitor
solid
solution
solve
  solved
  solving
some *(a portion)*
  [sum *(total)*]
somebody
someday
somehow
someone
something

sometime *(indefinite, unspecified)*
  [sometimes *(on some occasions, now and then)*]
somewhat
somewhere
son *(male offspring)*
  [sun *(a star)*]
song
soon
sore *(painful)*
  [soar *(fly)*]
sought
sorry
  sorrier
  sorriest
sort
soul *(spirit)*
  [sole *(1. only, 2. bottom of foot)*]
sound
soup
sour
source
south
South
South Africa
South Carolina
South Dakota
southeast
  southeastern
southern
southernmost
southwest
  southwestern
Soviet
sow *(plant seeds) (irreg. vb)*
  [sew *(mend)*]
  [so *(in order that)*]
sown

sp
space
  spaced
  spacing
  spacious
Spain
  Spaniard
  Spanish
spare

spared
sparing
spark
spasm
speak *(irreg. vb)*
spear
special
species
specific
  specifically
specify
  specified
  specifies
speech
  speeches
speed
  sped, speeded
speedy
  speedier
  speediest
  speediness
spell
spend *(irreg. vb)*
spent
sphere
spider
spill
  spilled, spilt
spin *(irreg. vb)*
  spinner
  spinning
spiral
spirit
spit *(irreg. vb)*
spite
splash
  splashes
split *(irreg. vb)*
  splitting
spoil
  spoilt
spoke *(1. did speak, 2. part of a wheel)*
spoken
spoon
sport
sports
spot
  spotted
  spotting

sprang
spread *(irreg. vb)*
spring *(irreg. vb)*
sprinkle
spun
sprung

sq

square
  squared
  squaring
squeak
squeeze
  squeezed
  squeezing
squirm
squirrel
squirt

st

stab
  stabbed
  stabbing
stability
  stabilities
stabilize
  stabilized
  stabilizer
  stabilizing
stable
  stabler
  stablest
stack
stadium
staff
stage
  staged
  staging
staid *(proper)*
  [stayed *(remained)*]
stain
stair *(a step)*
  [stare *(look intently)*]
stake *(post)*
  [steak *(slice of beef)*]
stall
stamp

stand *(irreg. vb)*
standard
stanza
star
  starred
  starring
  starry
starboard
stardom
stardust
stare *(look intently)*
  [stair *(a step)*]
  stared
  staring
starfish
starry
  starrier
  starriest
start
state
  stated
  stating
statement
station
stationary *(in a fixed position)*
  [stationery *(writing paper)*]
statistic
  statistical
  statistically
  statistician
statue
stay *(remained)*
  [staid *(proper)*]
steady
  steadied
  steadier
  steadies
  steadiest
  steadily
  steadiness
steak *(slice of beef)*
  [stake *(post)*]
steal *(rob) (irreg. vb)*
  [steel *(metal)*]
steam
  steamy
steel *(metal)*
  [steal *(rob)*]

The following regular endings are not in the word list & can be added to the root word without changes: -s -ed -ing -er -est -ly -ful -less -ness. Most exceptions & root changes are in the list.

steep
steeple
steer
stem
  stemmed
  stemming
step *(walk)*
  [steppe *(prairie of
  Europe or Asia)*]
  stepped
  stepping
stereo
stereotype
  stereotypical
stern
stick *(irreg. vb)*
  sticky
stiff
stile *(gate)*
  [style *(fashion)*]
still
sting
stir
  stirred
  stirring
stitch
  stitches
stock
  stocked
  stocking
stole
stolen
stomach
stone
  stoned
  stoning
stood
stop
  stopped
  stopper
  stopping
store
  stored
  storing
storm
  stormy
story
  stories
stove
straight *(not crooked)*
  [strait *(channel of
  water)*]
strain

strait *(channel of water)*
  [straight *(not
  crooked)*]
strange
  stranger
  strangest
strategy
  strategies
straw
streak
stream
streamline
streamlined
  streamliner
street
strength
  strengthen
stress
  stresses
stressful
stretch
  stretches
stride *(irreg. vb)*
  striding
strike *(irreg. vb)*
  striker
  striking
string *(irreg. vb)*
strip
  stripped
  stripper
  stripping
strode
stroke
  stroked
  stroking
strong
struck
structure
  structured
  structuring
struggle
  struggled
  struggling
strung
stubborn
stuck
student
study
  studied
stuff
stung
stupid

style *(fashion)*
  [stile *(gate)*]
  styled
  styling

su

subject
submarine
  submariner
submerge
  submerged
  submerging
submerse
  submersed
  submersing
subset
subtle
  subtler
  subtlest
  subtly
  subtlety
  subtleties
substance
substitute
  substituted
  substituting
  substitution
subtract
subtraction
succeed
success
  successes
  succession
  successive
  successor
succinct
succumb
such
sudden
sue
suffer
suffice
  sufficed
  sufficing
sufficient
suffix
  suffixes
sugar
  sugary
suggest
  suggestion
  suggestive

suit
suitable
  suitably
  suitability
suite *(connected rooms)*
  [sweet *(sugary)*]
sum *(total)*
  [some *(portion)*]
  summed
  summing
summer
sun *(star)*
  [son *(male offspring)*]
  sunned
  sunning
Sunday
sung
sunk
sunlight
sunny
  sunnier
  sunniest
sunrise
sunset
sunshine
suntan
  suntanned
  suntanning
super
superficial
superior
supermarket
supersede
  superseded
  superseding
supervise
  supervision
  supervisor
  supervisory
supine
supper
supply
  supplied
  supplier
  supplies
support
suppose *(verb)*
  [supposed *(adjective)*]

supposing
supreme
sure
  surer
  surest
surf *(ocean waves)*
  [serf *(feudal servant)*]
surface
  surfaced
  surfacing
surprise
  surprised
  surprising
surround
survey
  surveyor
survive
  survived
  surviving
  survivor
  survival
suspect

sw

swallow
swam
swamp
swang
swear *(irreg. vb)*
sweat
sweater
Swede
  Sweden
sweep
sweet *(sugary)*
  [suite *(connected rooms)*]
  sweeten
swell
swept
swift
swim *(irreg. vb)*
  swimmer
  swimming
swing *(irreg. vb)*
  swinger
  swinging
Swiss

Switzerland
switch
  switches
sword
swore
sworn
swum
swung

sy

syllable
syllabication
symbol *(sign)*
  [cymbal *(percussion instrument)*]
sympathetic
  sympathetically
sympathy
  sympathies
  sympathize
symphony
  symphonies
symptom
  symptomatic
synagogue
synonym
  synonymous
Syria
system
systematic
  systematically

ta

table
tacks *(flat-headed nails)*
  [tax *(money paid to government)*]
tag
  tagged
  tagging
tail *(animal's hind appendage)*
  [tale *(story)*]
  tailless
tailor
take *(irreg. vb)*
  taking

The following regular endings are not in the word list & can be added to the root word without changes: -s -ed -ing -er -est -ly -ful -less -ness. Most exceptions & root changes are in the list.

taken
tale *(story)*
  [tail *(animal's hind appendage)*]
talk
tall
tank
tap
  tapped
  tapping
tape
  taped
  taping
taps *(bugle call)*
tar
tardy
target
tart
task
taste
  tasted
  taster
  tasting
taught *(did teach)*
  [taut *(tight)*]
tax *(money paid to government)*
  [tacks *(flat-headed nails)*]
  taxes

te

tea *(a hot drink)*
  [tee *(holder for golf balls)*]
teach *(irreg. vb)*
  teaches
team *(crew)*
  [teem *(swarm)*]
tear *(water from eye)*
  [tier *(row)*]
tear *(irreg. vb)*
tease *(mock)*
  [teas *(hot drinks)*]
  [tees *(holders for golf balls)*]
teaspoon
technical
technique
tee *(holder for golf balls)*
  [tea *(a hot drink)*]
teem *(swarm)*

[team *(crew)*]
teenage
  teenager
teeth
teetotal
telecast
telecommunication
telegram
  telegrammed
  telegramming
telephone
  telephoned
  telephoning
telescope
  telescoped
  telescoping
televise
  televised
  televising
  television
tell *(irreg. vb)*
temperament
  temperamental
temperature
temporary
  temporarily
temple
tempt
ten
  tenth
tenant
tend
tendency
  tendencies
tender
Tennessee
tense
  tensed
  tensing
tent
tenth
term
tern *(sea bird)*
  [turn *(rotate)*]
terrible
terrific
territory
  territorial
  territories
terror
test
Texas
texture

textured
texturing

th

than *(conjunction)*
  [then *(adverb)*]
thank
Thanksgiving
that
the
theater
  theatrical
thee
their *(belonging to them)*
  [there *(at that place)*]
  [they're *(they are)*]
theirs *(belonging to them)*
  [there's *(contraction of there is)*]
them
theme
themselves
then *(adverb)*
  [than *(conjunction)*]
theory
there *(at that place)*
  [their *(belonging to them)*]
  [they're *(contraction of they are)*]
there's *(contraction of there is)*
  [theirs *(belonging to them)*]
therefore
thermometer
thermonuclear
these
they
they'd *(contraction of they would)*
they'll *(contraction of they will)*
they're *(contraction of they are)*
  [their *(belonging to them)*]
  [there *(at that place)*]
thick
thief
thin
  thinned

thinner
thinness
thinnest
thinning
thing
think *(irreg. vb)*
third
thirsty
thirteen
  thirteenth
thirty
  thirties
  thirtieth
this
thorough
those
thou
though
thought
thousand
  thousandfold
  thousandth
thread
threat
three
threw *(tossed)*
  [through *(finished)*]
thrill
throat
throne *(king's chair)*
  [thrown *(tossed)*]
through *(finished)*
  [threw *(tossed)*]
throughout
throw *(irreg. vb)*
thrown *(tossed)*
  [throne *(king's chair)*]
thrust
thumb
thunder
Thursday
thus
thy
thyme *(herb)*
  [time *(past, present and future)*

ti

tic *(twitch)*

[tick *(1. insect, 2. clock sound)*)]
ticket
  ticketed
  ticketing
tickle
tide *(ebb and flow)*
  [tied *(bound)*]
tie
  tied *(bound)*
  [tide *(ebb and flow)*]
  tying
tier *(a row)*
  [tear *(water from eye)*]
tiger
tight
till
timber
time *(past, present and future)*
  [thyme *(herb)*]
  timed
  timer
  timing
  timely
  timelier
  timeliest
  timeliness
timetable
timeworn
timid
  timidity
tin
  tinned
  tinning
tinder
tinderbox
tinfoil
tinge
  tinged
tiny
  tinier
  tiniest
tip
  tipped
  tipper
  tipping
tire
  tired
  tireless

tiredness
tiring
tiresome
tissue
title
  titled
  titling

to

to *(toward)*
  [too *(also)*]
  [two *(the number 2)*]
toad *(froglike animal)*
  [towed *(pulled)*]
tobacco
today
toe *(digit on foot)*
  [tow *(pull)*]
together
  togetherness
told *(informed)*
  [tolled *(rang)*]
tomorrow
ton
tone
tongue
  tongued
  tonguing
tonic
tonight
too *(also)*
  [to *(toward)*]
  [two *(the number 2)*]
took
tool
tooth
top
  topped
  topper
  topping
topic
topical
topple
  toppled
  toppling
tore
torn
torture
  tortured

The following regular endings are not in the word list & can be added to the root word without changes: -s -ed -ing -er -est -ly -ful -less -ness. Most exceptions & root changes are in the list.

torturer
torturing
toss
total
touch
  touches
  touchy
  touchier
  touchiest
tough
tow *(pull)*
  [toe *(digit on foot)*]
toward
towed *(pulled)*
  [toad *(froglike animal)*]
tower
town
township
townspeople
toxic
  toxicity
toy

tr

trace
  traced
  tracer
  tracing
track
trade
  traded
  trader
  trading
tradition
  traditional
traffic
tragedy
  tragedies
tragic
  tragically
trail
train
transact
transatlantic
transform
translate
  translated
  translating
translator
  translation
transportation

trap
  trapped
  trapper
  trapping
travel
tray
treasure
  treasured
  treasurer
  treasuring
treat
treatment
treaty
  treaties
tree
  treed
  treelike
treetop
tremendous
trial
triangle
tribe
trick
  trickery
  tricky
tried
trim
  trimmed
  trimmer
  trimming
trip
  tripped
  tripping
troop *(military)*
  [troupe *(acting)*]
tropical
trouble
  troubled
  troubling
  troublesome
troupe *(acting)*
  [troop *(acting)*]
truck
true
  truer
  truest
  truly
trumpet
trunk
trust *(confidence)*
  [trussed *(tied up)*]
truth
try

tried
tries

tu

tub
tube
Tuesday
tug
tumble
tune
  tuned
  tuning
tunnel
turkey
Turkey
turn *(rotate)*
  [tern *(sea bird)*]
turtle

tw

twelve
  twelfth
twenty
  twenties
  twentieth
twice
twin
twist
two *(the number 2)*
  [to *(toward)*]
  [too *(also)*]

ty

type
  typed
  typing
typical

ug

ugly
  uglier
  ugliest
  ugliness

ul

ultimate

um
umbrella

un
unable
uncle
underground
underline
  underlined
  underlining
underneath
understand *(irreg. vb)*
underwater
unexpected
unhappy
  unhappily
  unhappiness
uniform
  uniformity
union
unique
unit
unite
  united
  uniting
United States
unity
universe
  universal
  universality
university
  universities
unkind
unknown
unless
unlike
unload
unlucky
unnecessary
unofficial
unrest
until
unusual
unwind *(irreg. vb)*

up
up

upbeat
upbringing
upcoming
update
upend
  upended
  upending
upheaval
upholster
upon
upper
upright
upset
  upsetting
upstairs
upward

ur
uranium
urge
  urged
  urging
urgent
urn *(vase)*
  [earn *(work for)*
Uruguay

us
us
use
  usage
  used
  using
usual

ut
Utah

va
vacant
vacation
vacuum
vague
vain *(conceited)*
  [vane *(wind indicator)*]

[vein *(blood vessel)*]
vale *(valley)*
  [veil *(face covering)*]
vary *(change)*
  [very *(much, greatly)*]

ve
vein *(blood vessel)*
  [vain *(conceited)*]
  [vane *(wind indicator)*]
Venezuela
Venus
verb
  verbal
verbalize
  verbalized
  verbalizing
Vermont
verse
  versed
version
versus
vertical
very *(much; greatly)*
  [vary *(change)*]
vessel

vi
vial *(jar)*
  [vile *(bad)*]
vibrate
  vibrated
  vibrating
  vibration
vice *(bad habit)*
  [vise *(a clamp)*]
victim
victory
  victories
  victorious
view
vile *(bad)*
  [vial *(jar)*]
village
  villager

The following regular endings are not in the word list & can be added to the root word without changes: -s -ed -ing -er -est -ly -ful -less -ness. Most exceptions & root changes are in the list.

villain
violate
  violated
  violating
  violation
violent
  violence
violet
violin
virgin
Virginia
  Virginian
vise *(a clamp)*
  vice *(bad habit)*
visible
  visibly
vision
  visionary
visit
  visitor
vitamin

vo

vocabulary
  vocabularies
vocation
voice
  voiced
  voicing
volcano
  volcanos
volume
volunteer
  voluntary
vote
  voted
  voter
  voting
vowel
voyage
  voyaged
  voyager
  voyaging

wa

wade *(walk in water)*
  [weighed
  *(measured
  heaviness)*]
wage
  waged

waging
wagon
wail *(cry)*
  [whale *(sea
  mammal)*]
waist *(middle of body)*
  [waste *(unused parts)*]
wait *(linger)*
  [weight *(heaviness)*]
waiter
  waitress
waive *(give up rights)*
  [wave *(signal hello or
  good-bye)*]
wake
  waked
  waking
walk
wall
wander
want *(desire)*
  [wont *(custom)*]
war
ware *(pottery)*
  [wear *(have on body)*]
  [where *(what place)*]
warm
  warmth
warn
warrior
was
wash
  washes
Washington
  Washingtonian
wasn't *(was not)*
waste *(unused parts)*
  [waist *(middle of
  body)*]
  wasted
  wasting
  wasteful
watch
  watches
water
wave *(signal hello or
  good-bye)*
  [waive *(give up right)*]
  waved
  waving
wax
  waxes
way *(road)*

[weigh *(measure
heaviness)*]
[whey *(watery part of
milk)*]

we

we *(us)*
  [wee *(small)*]
wear *(irreg. vb)*
weather *(climate)*
  [whether *(if)*]
weave *(irreg. vb)*
  [we've *(we have)*]
Wednesday
weed *(a plant)*
  [we'd *(we would)*]
week *(seven days)*
  [weak *(not strong)*]
weekend
weep *(irreg. vb)*
weigh *(measure
  heaviness)*
  [way *(road)*]
  [whey *(watery part of
  milk)*]
weighed
  *(measure
  heaviness)*
  [wade *(walk in water)*]
weight *(heaviness)*
  [wait *(linger)*]
weir *(dam)*
  [we're *(we are)*]
welcome
  welcomed
  welcoming
well
we'll *(we will)*
  [weal *(well-being)*]
  [wheel *(circular
  frame)*]
went
wept
were
we're *(we are)*
  [weir *(dam)*]
weren't *(were not)*
west
  western
  westward
West Virginia
wet *(moist) (irreg. vb)*

[whet *(sharpen)*]
wetted
wetter
wettest
wetting
we've *(we have)*
[weave *(interlace)*]

wh

whale *(sea mammal)*
[wail *(cry)*]
whaling
what
whatever
wheat
wheel *(circular frame)*
[weal *(well-being)*]
[we'll *(we will)*]
when
whenever
where *(what place)*
[ware *(pottery)*]
[wear *(have on body)*]
wherever
whet *(sharpen)*
[wet *(moist)*]
whether *(if)*
[weather *(climate)*]
whey *(watery part of milk)*
[way *(road)*]
[weigh *(measure heaviness)*]
which *(what one)*
[witch *(sorceress)*]
while *(during)*
[wile *(a trick)*]
whine *(complain and cry)*
[wine *(a drink)*]
whip
whipped
whipping
whisper
whistle
whistled
whistling
white
whited
whiten
whiter

whitest
whitewash
whiz
whizzed
whizzing
who
whoever
whole *(complete)*
[hole *(an opening)*]
wholly *(completely)*
[holey *(full of holes)*]
[holy *(sacred)*]
whom
whose *(who owns)*
[who's *(who is)*]
who's *(who is)*
[whose *(who owns)*]
why

wi

wicked
wide
widen
wider
widest
width
wife
wives
wild
wilderness
wile *(a trick)*
[while *(during)*]
will
win
winner
winning
wind *(irreg. vb)*
window
wine *(a drink)*
[whine *(cry and complain)*]
wing
winged
winging
wingless
wink
winter
wipe
wiped

wiper
wiping
wire
wired
wiring
Wisconsin
wise
wiser
wisest
wish
wishes
wit
witch *(sorceress)*
[which *(what one)*]
witches
with
withdraw
withdrawal
withdrawn
withhold
within
without
withstand
witness
wittingly
witty
wittier
wittiest
wittily
wittiness
wizard
wizardry

wo

wobble
wobbled
wobbling
woe
woebegone
woke
wolf
wolves
wolfish
woman *(one female)*
[women *(several females)*]
won *(triumphed)*
[one *(the number 1)*]
wonder

The following regular endings are not in the word list & can be added to the root word without changes: -s -ed -ing -er -est -ly -ful -less -ness. Most exceptions & root changes are in the list.

wondrous
wonderland
wont (*custom*)
   [want (*desire*)]
won't (*would not*)
wood (*of a tree*)
   [would (*is willing to*)]
woodchuck
woodland
woodpile
woodshed
woodsy
woodwork
wool
   woolen
   woollier
   woolliest
word
   wordy
   wordier
   wordiest
wore
work
   workable
workshop
world
   worldlier
   worldliest
   worldliness
worm
worn
worry
   worried
   worrier
worse
   worsen
worship
   worshipped
   worshipper
   worshipping
worst (*most bad*)
   [wurst (*sausage*)]
worth
worthy
worthwhile
would (*is willing to*)
   [wood (*of a tree*)]
wouldn't (*would not*)
wound
wove
   woven

wr

wrap (*cover*)
   [rap (*hit*)]
   wrapped
   wrapping
wreak (*inflict*)
   [reek (*give off strong odor*)]
wreck
wrench
   wrenches
wrest (*take from*)
   [rest (*relax*)]
wring (*squeeze*) (*irreg. vb*)
   [ring (*circular band*)]
write (*inscribe*) (*irreg. vb*)
   [right (*correct*)]
   rite (*ceremony*)]
   written
   writing
   writer
wrong
wrote (*did write*)
   [rote (*by memory*)]
wrung (*squeezed*)
   [rung (*step on a ladder*)]
wurst (*sausage*)
   [worst (*most bad*)]
wry (*ironically humorous*)
   [rye (*grain*)]
Wyoming

x

x-ray

xy

xylophone

ya

yacht
yard
yarn

ye

year

yell
yellow
   yellowish
yelp
yes
   yeses
yesterday
yesteryear
yet
yew (*a shrub*)
   [ewe (*female sheep*)]
   [you (*yourself*)]

yo

yoke (*harness*)
   [yolk (*egg center*)]
you (*yourself*)
   [ewe (*female sheep*)]
   [yew (*a shrub*)]
you'd (*you would*)
you'll (*you will*)
   [yule (*Christmas*)]
you're (*you are*)
   [your (*belonging to you*)]
you've (*you have*)
young
   younger
   youngest
your (*belonging to you*)
   [you're (*you are*)]
yours
yourself
youth

yu

Yugoslavia
yule (*Christmas*)
   you'll (*you will*)

ze

zeal
   zealous
zebra
zero
   zeroed
   zeroing
   zeroes

zest
zestful

zi
zip
   zipped
   zipping
   zipper

zo
zone
   zoned
   zoning
zoo
   zookeeper
   zoology

The following regular endings are not in the word list & can be added to the root word without changes: -s -ed -ing -er -est -ly -ful -less -ness. Most exceptions & root changes are in the list.

SPELLING RULES

PLURALS AND "S" FORM OF VERBS
(The more important rules have capital letters and bold-faced type.)

A. **Add "s" to most nouns and verbs. ex. cows, runs** *(Note: These are still one syllable after "s" is added.)*

B. **Add "es" if the word ends in "ch", "sh", "x", "s", or "z". ex. box - boxes, church - churches.** *(Note: These are two syllable words when "es" is added.)*

For words ending in "y"

C. **If the word ends in a "y", preceded by a consonant, change the "y" to "i" and add "es". ex. baby - babies, city - cities**

d. Note: Don't change "y" if a vowel preceded it. ex. key - keys

e. Also don't change "y" if it is a proper noun. ex. one Kathy - two Kathys

For words ending in "o"

f. For a few words ending in "o" add "es". ex. go - goes

g. However, for a lot of words ending in "o", just adding an "s" is OK because either spelling is correct. ex. banjo or banjoes

h. If the "o" is preceded by a vowel, just add "s" ex. radio - radios

For words ending in "f"

i. For a few nouns ending in "f" (or "fe"), change the "f" to "v" and add "es". ex. leaf - leaves, wife - wives.

Other Plurals

j. Some foreign nouns have different plurals. ex. alumnus - alumni, index - indices

k. A few English nouns have different plurals. ex. foot - feet

l. A few nouns don't change for plurals. ex. deer - deer

m. Symbols form plurals with apostrophe " 's " ex. 2's, ABC's

ADDING SUFFIXES

Basic Rule: Just add the suffix, except as follows:

Regular examples: want - wanted, wanting, wants (Important: See plurals list)

For words ending in "e"

A. **Drop the final "e" if the suffix begins with a vowel. ex. rose - rosy, name - naming, named**

b. Keep the final "e" if the suffix begins with a consonant. ex. safe - safely

c. Keep the final "e" if a vowel preceded it. ex. see - seeing

d. Drop the final "le" if the suffix is "ly" (no double "l"). ex. able - ably

For words ending in "y"

E. **Change the "y" to "i" if "y" is preceded by a consonant. ex. carry - carried (Suffix here is "-ed")**

f. Don't change the "y" to "i" if "y" is preceded by a vowel. ex. joy - joyful

g. Don't change the "y" to "i" if the suffix begins with an "i". ex. carry - carrying (Suffix here is "-ing")

For words ending in "c"

h.   Add a "k" before any suffix beginning with an "e", "i" or "y". ex. picnic - picnicking, panic - panicky

Doubling the final letter

I.   **Double the final consonant before adding the suffix if:**

      1. the word has one syllable (or the final syllable is accented)

      2. the word ends in a single consonant (not "x")

      3. the word has a single vowel letter

      4. the suffix begins with a vowel

      Examples: brag - bragged, (not "x", box - boxing)

j.   You do not double the final consonant (Basic Rule applies) if:

      1. the suffix begins with a consonant. ex bag - bagful

      2. the vowel has two letters. ex. rain - rained

      3. the word has two final consonants. ex. hard - harder

      4. the final syllable is not accented. ex. benefit - benefited

k.   If the word has two syllables and is accented on the last syllable, treat it as one syllable word. (See I. and j. above.) ex. admit - admittance

l.   If the word has two syllables and is accented on the first syllable, do not double the last letter (back to Basic Rule). ex. equal - equaled

m.   The final "l" is kept when adding "ly". (This really restated the Basic Rule I. and j., but it looks funny when you see two "l's".) ex. cool - coolly

PREFIXES

Basic Rule: Prefixes never change spelling, they just add on.

a.   Even if it means having double letters. ex. misspell, illegible

b.   Often the prefix "ex" and "self" use a hyphen. ex. ex-resident, self-help

"EI" OR "IE" RULE (of dubious value)

Basic Rule: Write "i" before "e", except after "c".

    Example: chief, believe.

a.   If the vowel sounds like long "a", spell it "ei". ex. neighbor, weigh

b.   **There are plenty of exceptions.** ex. their, Neil, science, either, leisure

COMPOUND WORDS

Basic Rule: Keep the full spelling of both words. Don't use a hyphen.

    Example: ear + ring = earring; room + mate = roommate

A more common usage or more specific meaning tends to put two words into a compound. ex. blackbird (one word), black car (two words)

SPELLING USING PHONICS

A lot of people think phonics rules are useful in learning to read, and they are. But phonics is also important in learning to spell because the sound-letter (phoneme-grapheme) correspondence works both ways. It is unfortunate that there are so many exceptions or variations on sound-letter correspondence (phonics isn't perfect), but there are plenty of words and parts of words that are spelled regularly. Look over the following two charts for vowels and consonants. If you know that much phonics, you will be able to spell many words and parts of words correctly.

You might say that the letter-sound correspondences in these two charts are a set of Spelling Rules based on phonics. Young children use invented spelling, which is really a kind of partial knowledge of phonics. As children get older, or writers mature, they still use invented spelling sometimes and their invented spelling is better because they know more phonics, plus they have learned the spelling of many letter clusters.

The following charts can also help you look up words in the Spelling Checker word list. If you can sound out a word (know the phonemes), you can look up their common and less common spellings in the charts.

All vowels and some consonants have more than one way to be spelled. Three consonant letters, C, Q, and X, have no sound (phoneme) of their own. The letter C makes either a /k/ or a /s/ sound. The letter C generally makes the /s/ sound before I, E, and Y, and it makes the /k/ sound before A, O, and U. The letter Q always appears with a U, and QU makes the /kw/ sound. The letter X usually makes the /ks/ sound.

The letter G can be sounded like a /g/ or a /j/. The letter S can make a /z/ or an /s/sound. The letter S makes the /z/ sound only at the end of some words. The digraph TH has two sounds: voiced as in "them" and unvoiced as in "thin".

The letter Y is a consonant at the beginning of most words and a vowel in the middle or end of a word. See Vowel Exceptions in charts.

Most linguists and dictionaries say that the digraph WH really represents the /hw/ blend, but this is a highly technical point lost on most spellers and speakers of English. The same is true for the digraph NG that is a unique phoneme /ng/.

The schwa sound is the unaccented vowel sound that sounds a good bit like a short /u/. It is helpful to remember that to have an unaccented vowel the word must also have at least one other accented vowel sound.

A blend is two different phonemes that occur together so that each is sounded, for example the "BL" as in "black". This is different from a consonant digraph like "SH", which makes its own phoneme. It is not a blend of /s/ and /h/. The Digraphs are in the charts.

Last, but not least, it is painful to remember that there are plenty of exceptions to the amount of phonics presented in the vowel and consonant charts. And that is why you have to learn to spell many words by "sight" or the whole word approach. It is also why the Spelling Checker word list should be your constant companion when writing anything.

If you are interested in spelling lessons, see the Spelling Book listed on the inside back cover.

VOWEL SOUNDS (alphabetical)

Phoneme		Common Spelling	Less Common Spelling
A Short	ă	A hat	
A Long	ā	A-E age, aid	EIGH eight, AY say, A (R) vary, AI (R) fair
A Broad	ä	A (R) far	A father
E Short	ĕ	E red	EA head
E Long	ē	E repay, EE see	EA seat, Y crazy
I Short	ĭ	I bit	Y gym
I Long	ī	I-E ice, Y try, I child	
O Short	ŏ	O hot	A watch
O Long	ō	O so, O-E nose	OA boat, OW know
O Broad	ô	O (R) for	A (L) all, A (U) auto A (W) awful
OI + OY	oy	OI boil, OY boy	
OU + OW	ou	OU out, OW owl	
OO Long	ōō, ü	OO moon	U ruby, EW chew
OO Short	ŏŏ, ů	OO good	U (L) pull, playful
U Short	ŭ	U nut	
U Long	ū	U-E use, U music	
∂ Schwa	∂	A alone, E taken, I direct, OU generous	
		O riot, U campus	

(The schwa phoneme is the unaccented vowel sound so it must be a polysyllable word.)

VOWEL SOUNDS (clustered)

Short Vowels

a - at   / ă /
e - end   / ĕ /
i - is   / ĭ /
o - hot   / ŏ /
u - up   / ŭ /

Long Vowels
Open Syllable Rule

a - baby / ā /
e - we   / ē /
i - idea / ī /
o - so   / ō /

Long Vowels
Final E Rule

a - make / ā /
e - here / ē /
i - five / ī /
o - home / ō /
u - use   / ū /

Long Vowel
Digraphs

ai - aid   / ā /
ay - say   / ā /
ea - eat   / ē /
ee - see   / ē /
oa - oat   / ō /
ow - own   / ō /

Schwa

u - hurt   / ∂ /
e - happen / ∂ /
o - other   / ∂ /

Vowel Y

y - try   / ī /
y - funny / ē /

Vowel Plus R

er - her   / r /
ir - sir   / r /
ur - fur   / r /
ar - far   / är /
ar - vary   / ār /
or - for   / ôr /

Dipthongs

oi - oil   / oi /
oy - boy   / oi /
ou - out   / ou /
ow - how   / ou /

Double O

oo - soon   / o͞o /
oo - good   / o͝o /
u - truth   / o͞o /
u - put   / o͝o /

Broad O

o - long   / ô /
a (l) - also / ô /
a (w) - saw / ô /
a (u) - auto / ô /

Vowel Exceptions

ea - bread	/ ĕ /	"ea" makes both a long and a short E sound.
e (silent) - come		E at the end of a word is usually silent and sometimes makes the preceding vowel long.
y - yes	/ y /	y is a consonant at the beginning of a word. (yes)
		y is long I in a one syllable word or middle. (cycle)
		y is long E at the end of a polysyllable word. (funny)
le - candle	/ ∂l /	final LE makes a schwa plus L sound.
al - pedal	/ ∂l /	final AL makes a schwa plus L sound also.
ul - awful	/ ∂l /	final UL makes a schwa plus L sound also.

CONSONANT SOUNDS (alphabetical)

Phoneme	Common Spelling	Less Common Spelling
B	B boy	
[C]	(No "C" phoneme; see K & S)	
CH	CH cheese	T nature
D	D dog	
F	F fat	PH phone
G	G girl	
H	H hot	
J	J just G giant	
K	C cat K king	CK sick CH chrome
KS	X fox (No "X" phoneme)	
KW	QU quick (No "Q" phoneme)	
L	L look	
M	M me	
N	N no	KN knife
NG	NG sing	
P	P put	
[Q]	(No "Q" phoneme; see KW)	
R	R run	WR write
S	S sit C city	
SH	SH shut TI action	
T	T toy	
TH (voiced)	TH this	
TH (voiceless)	TH thing	
V	V voice	
W	W will	
WH	WH white	
[X]	(No "X" phoneme; see KS)	
Y (consonant)	Y yes	I onion
Z	S is Z zero	
ZH	SI vision	S pleasure

CONSONANT SOUNDS (clustered)

Single Consonants

b	h	n	v
c	j	p	w
d	k	r	y
f	l	s	z
g	m	t	

Consonant Digraphs

ch as in "church"
sh as in "shoe"
th (voiced) as in "thin"
th (voiceless) as in "this"
wh (hw blend) as in "which"

Important Exceptions

qu = /kw/ blend as in "quick"
(the letter "q" is never used
without "u")
ph =/f/ sound as in "phone"
c = /s/ before "i, e or y", as in "city"
c = /k/ before a, o or u, as in "cat"
g = /j/ before i, e, or y, as in "gem"
g = /g/ before a, o, or u, as in "good"
x = /ks/ blend as in "fox"
s = /z/ sound at the end of some
words as in "is"
ng = /ng/ unique phoneme, as
in "sing"

Rare Exceptions

ch = /k/ as in "character"
ch = /sh/ as in "chef"
ti = /sh/ as in "attention"
s = /sh/ as in "sure"
x = /gz/ as in "exact"
s = /zh/ as in "measure"
si = /zh/ as in "vision"

Silent Consonants

gn = /n/ as in "gnat"
kn = /n/ as in "knife"
wr = /r/ as in "write"
gh = /-/ as in "right"
ck = /k/ as in "back"
mb = /m/ as in "lamb"
lf = /f/ as in "calf"
lk = /k/ as in "walk"
tle = /-/ as in "castle"

Beginning Consonant Blends

(r family)	(l family)	(s family)	(3 letter)	(no family)
br	bl	sc	scr	dw
cr	cl	sk	squ	tw
dr	fl	sm	str	
fr	gl	sn	thr	
gr	pl	sp	spr	
pr	sl	st	spl	
tr		sw	shr	
wr			sch	

Final Consonant Blends

ct - act	**mp** - jump	**nt** - ant	**rk** - dark
ft - lift	**nc** (e) - since	**pt** - kept	**rt** - art
ld - old	**nd** - and	**rd** - hard	**st** - least
lt - salt	**nk** - ink		**sk** - risk

CAPITALIZATION

A. Capitalize all proper nouns

1. Names.
Example: George Washington.

2. Specific titles.
Example: George Washington, the President of the United States.

3. Countries, states, geographic areas.
Examples: France, Missouri, the East, the Sierras, Lake Erie, the Colorado (River)

4. Streets, roads, avenues.
Examples: Hill St., First Avenue.

5. Religious names and all pronouns relating to the entity.
Examples: God, Jesus Christ, His, Thine; Bible, Catholic, Jewish.

6. Days, months.
Examples: Thursday, April.

7. Schools.
Example: Dayton Valley High School, University of Southern California, Forest Elementary School.

8. Holidays.
Examples: Christmas, Memorial Day, Fourth of July.

9. Races.
Examples: Spanish, Indian.

10. Trade Names.
Example: Nabisco.

B. Capitalize the first word in a sentence.
Example: The men don't want to go to war.

C. Capitalize the first letter of the first word in each line of poetry.
Example:
"...If I were a dead leaf thou mightest bear,
If I were a swift cloud to fly with thee;
A wave to pant beneath thy power, and share ..."
(from "Ode to the West Wind", by Percy Shelley)

74

D. Capitalize all main words in a title.
Example: The new book is <u>The World Can Become a More Beautiful Place</u>.

E. Capitalize the first word in a quote.
Example: He said, "<u>I</u>f I can't have it, nobody will."

The tendency is to capitalize a word if there is doubt, such as if it is similar to a proper capitalization situation.

Do not capitalize:

1. Prepositions, articles, or conjunctions in a title unless these words have over four letters. <u>BUT</u> always capitalize verbs, no matter how small, and "to" as part of the infinitive verb form.
Example: We heard an interesting speech, "Homework <u>I</u>s <u>W</u>ithout Tears: How <u>T</u>o Make You <u>a</u>nd Your Child Choose <u>t</u>he Right Time".

2. Seasons.
Example: The frost was a sign that <u>w</u>inter was near.

3. Directions of the compass.
Example: Our friend's house was <u>w</u>est of town.

4. Words in quotations if only part of the quotation is used.
The principal had "<u>m</u>ixed <u>f</u>eelings" about the new school legislation.

5. The word is a general, not a specific, description of a person or thing. Note the title "president" and the words "high school" in the following example: The class president was the first one at the high school prom. But specific persons and titles are capitalized in the following example: President Jackson attended the Kansas City High School Prom.

75

PUNCTUATION

Period

1. At end of sentence. *ex. Birds fly*
2. After some Abbreviations. *ex. Mr., U.S.A.*
3. In decimal fractions. *ex. 5.95, 3.15*

Question Mark

1. At the end of question. *ex. Who is he?*
2. To express doubt. *ex. He weighs 250 (?) pounds.*

Apostrophe

1. To form possessive. *ex. Bill's bike*
2. Omitted letters or numbers. *ex. isn't, '93*
3. Plurals of symbols. *ex. 1960's, two A's (See expanded explanation of apostrophe use at the end of this section)*

Parenthesis

1. Supplementary material. *ex. The map (see illustration) is good.*
2. Stronger than commas. *ex. Joe (the bad guy) is dead.*
3. Enclose numbers. *ex. Her car is (1) a Ford, (2) too slow.*

Colon

1. Introduce a series. *ex. He has three things: money, brains, charm.*
2. Separate subtitles. *ex. The Book: How to Read It.*
3. Set off a clause. *ex. He's not heavy: he's my brother.*
4. Business letter salutation. *ex. Dear Sir:*
5. Times and ratios. *ex. 7:45 A.M., Mix it 3:1.*

Semicolon

1. Stronger than a comma. *ex. Peace is difficult; war is hell.*
2. Separate clauses containing commas. *ex. He was tired; therefore, he quit.*

Quotation Marks

1. Speech is dialogue. *ex. She said, "Hello".*
2. Titles. *ex. He read "Shane".*
3. Special words or slang. *ex. He is "nuts".*
4. Direct quote. *ex. He told me that he "never lied".*

Comma
1. Independent clauses. *ex. I like him, and he is tall.*
2. Dependent clause that precedes a main clause. *ex. After the game, we went home.*
3. Semi-parenthetical clause. *ex. Bill, the tall one, is here.*
4. Series. *ex. He likes candy, ice cream, and diamonds.*
5. Multiple adjectives. *ex. The big, bad, ugly wolf.*
6. In dialogue. *ex. She said, "Hello".*
7. Dates. *ex. July 4, 1776.*
8. Titles. *ex. Joe Smith, Ph.D.*
9. Informal letter salutation. *ex. Dear Mary,*
10. Letter closing. *ex. Yours truly,*
11. Inverted names. *ex. Smith, Joe.*
12. Separate city and state. *ex. Los Angeles, California.*
13. In numbers. *ex. 43, 126.*

Exclamation Point
1. Show strong emotion. *ex. She is the best!*
2. After interjections. *ex. Help!*

Dash
1. Show duration. *ex. 1949-50, Rome-London.*
2. Parenthetical material. *ex. The girl - the pretty one - is here.*
2. To show omissions. *ex. She called him a —.*

Ellipsis
1. To show omitted material. *ex. He....went home.*

APOSTROPHE

A.   Use an apostrophe to show possession.

1. For a singular possessive not ending in "s", add an apostrophe and "s".

Example: The student's book is lost.

2. For a possessive of plural ending in "s", add only an apostrophe after "s".

Example: There were many students' books lost.

3. For a possessive of the "singular" form of a word that ends in "s", add an apostrophe after the "s" or an apostrophe and the "s".

Example: "Cross": Mrs. Cross' or Mrs. Cross's.

4. To show joint possession, add apostrophe to the last of the names.

Example: John and Nancy: John and Nancy's house.

5. In compound words, add to last part of compound.

Examples: sister-in-law: Sister-in-law's. No one else: no one else's.

B.   Use an apostrophe to show omission

Letters, such as contractions, or numbers, such as years.

Examples:

> *cannot: can't*
>
> *of the clock: o'clock*
>
> *1959 Chevy: '59 Chevy*

C.   Use an apostrophe to show some plurals.

1.   For plurals or numbers, letters, and words.

Examples:

> *The 7's were the best.*
>
> *Be careful to make your a's readable.*
>
> *Circle all the and's in the paragraph.*
>
> *The Roaring '20's was a wild era.*

2.   Abbreviations that have periods.

Example:

> *The two men were Ph.D.'s.*

WHEN NOT TO USE AN APOSTROPHE

The problem is overuse of the apostrophe. The tendency is to throw it in wherever one sees an "s".

Do not use an apostrophe:

1. To indicate simply the plural

Examples:

The McKees are coming over tonight.

The two cats are both white.

2. With pronouns as its, hers, ours, whose.

Example: The purse is hers.

Note regarding "its" and "it's": only use an apostrophe when it indicated the contraction for "it is" or "it has".

ABBREVIATIONS

U.S. Post Office-Authorized State Abbreviations. (Note: No periods)

Alabama	AL
Alaska	AK
American Samoa	AS
Arizona	AZ
Arkansas	AR
California	CA
Canal Zone	CZ
Colorado	CO
Connecticut	CT
Delaware	DE
District of Columbia	DC
Florida	FL
Georgia	GA
Guam	GU
Hawaii	HI
Idaho	ID
Illinois	IL
Indiana	IN
Iowa	IA
Kansas	KS
Kentucky	KY
Louisiana	LA
Maine	ME
Maryland	MD
Massachusetts	MA
Michigan	MI
Minnesota	MN
Mississippi	MS
Missouri	MO
Montana	MT
Nebraska	NE
Nevada	NV
New Hampshire	NH
New Jersey	NJ
New Mexico	NM
New York	NY
North Carolina	NC
North Dakota	ND
Ohio	OH
Oklahoma	OK
Oregon	OR
Pennsylvania	PA
Puerto Rico	PR
Rhode Island	RI
South Carolina	SC
South Dakota	SD
Tennessee	TN
Texas	TX
Trust Territories	TT
Utah	UT
Vermont	VT
Virginia	VA
Virgin Islands	VI
Washington	WA
West Virginia	WV
Wisconsin	WI
Wyoming	WY

Also approved for use in addressing mail are the following street abbreviations:

Alley	Aly
Arcade	Arc
Boulevard	Blvd
Branch	Br
Bypass	Byp
Causeway	Cswy
Center	Ctr
Circle	Cir
Court	Ct
Courts	Cts
Crescent	Cres
Drive	Dr
Expressway	Expy
Extended	Ext
Extension	Ext
Freeway	Fwy
Gardens	Gdns
Grove	Grv
Heights	Hts
Highway	Hwy
Lane	Ln
Manor	Mnr
Place	Pl
Plaza	Plz
Point	Pt
Road	Rd
Rural	R
Square	Sq
Street	St
Terrace	Ter
Trail	Trl
Turnpike	Tpke
Viaduct	Via
Vista	Vis

Titles

Mister	Mr.
Married Woman	Mrs.
Unmarried Woman	Miss
Any Woman	Ms.
Doctor	Dr.
Reverend	Rev.
Father	Fr.
Senator	Sen.
Representative	Rep.
Honorable (judge)	Hon.
Governor	Gov.
President	Pres.
Vice President	V.P.

Time

Before noon (ante meridian)	A.M. or a.m.
After noon (post meridian)	P.M. or p.m.
Eastern Standard Time	EST
Eastern Daylight Time	EDT
Central Standard Time	CST
Central Daylight Time	CDT
Mountain Standard Time	MST
Mountain Daylight Time	MDT
Pacific Standard Time	PST
Pacific Daylight Time	PDT
Greenwich Mean Time	GMT
Minute	min.
Second	sec.

Scholarly Degrees and Titles of Respect

Bachelor of Arts	B.A.
Bachelor of Science	B.S.
Doctor of Dental Surgery	D.D.S.
Master of Arts	M.A.
Doctor of Medicine	M.D.
Doctor of Philosophy	Ph.D.
Bachelor of Law	L.L.B.
Certified Public Accountant	C.P.A.

Months

January	Jan.
February	Feb.
March	Mar.
April	Apr.
May	May
June	June
July	July
August	Aug.
September	Sept.
October	Oct.
November	Nov.
December	Dec.

Days of the Week

Sunday	Sun.
Monday	Mon.
Tuesday	Tue.
Wednesday	Wed.
Thursday	Thur.
Friday	Fri.
Saturday	Sat.
Sunday	Sun.

Measurements

Standard (U.S.)
(Note - use period)

Length

inch	in.
foot	ft.
yard	yd.
rod	r.
furlong	fur.
mile	mi.

Capacity liquid

ounce	oz.
pint	pt.
quart	qt.
gallon	gal.
barrel	bb.

Capacity dry

pint	pt.
quart	qt.
peck	pk.
bushel	bu.

Weight

dram	dr.
ounce	oz.
pound	lb.
hundredweight	hwt.
ton	t.

Temperature

fahrenheit	F

Metric
(Note - no period)

Length

millimeter	mm	.001
centimeter	cm	.01
decimeter	dm	.1
meter	m	1.
decameter	dkm	10.
hectometer	hm	100.
kilometer	km	1000.

Capacity

milliliter	ml	.001
centiliter	cl	.01
deciliter	dl	.1
liter	l	1.
decaliter	dkl	10.
hectoliter	hl	100.
kiloliter	kl	1000.

Weight

milligram	mg	.001
centigram	cg	.01
decigram	dg	.1
gram	g	1.
decagram	dkg	10.
hectogram	hg	100.
kilogram	kg	1000.

Temperature

centigrade	C
celsius	C

Parts of Speech

adjective .... adj.
adverb .... adv.
conjunction .... conj.
interjection .... inter.
noun .... n.
preposition .... prep.
pronoun .... pron.
verb .... vb.
(For explanations of Parts of Speech, see page 93)

Reference Abbreviations
Commonly Used

cont. .... continued
etc. (Latin) .... *et cetera*, and so forth
    (in speech, etc. is pronounced et-SET-uh-ruh)
i.e. (Latin) .... id est, it is
misc. .... miscellaneous
p. .... page
pp .... pages
PS (Latin) .... *postscriptum*, postscript
PPS (Latin) .... *post postscriptum*, a later
                                      postscript
vol. .... volume
ex. or Ex. .... example

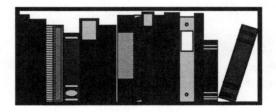

GRAMMAR

SENTENCES - BASIC CONSTRUCTION

Part of grammar (rules on language use) is about different types of sentences. This is also called syntax. Here is a simplified explanation of some different types of common sentences:

Minimum sentence:
The basic rule is that every sentence must have a noun (or pronoun) and a verb. Hence the minimum sentence looks like this.
Birds fly.
Subject + predicate *or*
Noun + verb.

Typical sentence:
Most sentences have another major part called the object which comes after the verb.
Birds fly home.
Subject + predicate + object *or*
Noun + verb + noun.

Modifying the subject:
Each part of a sentence can be modified by adding another word or words. *For example:*
The big black birds fly home.
Modified subject + predicate + object *or*
Article + adjective + adjective + noun + verb + noun.

Modifying the Predicate:
Birds rapidly fly home.
Subject + modified predicate + object *or*
Noun + adverb + verb + noun.

Modifying the object:
Birds fly to old homes.
Subject + predicate + modified object *or*
Noun + verb + preposition + adjective + noun.
Or you can put the whole thing together:
The big black birds rapidly fly to their old homes.

Negative sentence

You can also make the sentence say the opposite or negative by adding a word or two like "no" or "not".

No birds fly.
Birds do not fly.

Questions

The usual way to make a sentence into a question is to put a verb in front of the subject and add a question mark at the end instead of a period. *For example:*

Is he fat?

Questions also frequently begin with one of the "W's" - Who, What, Why, When, Where, Which (or How). *For example:*

What birds fly?
How do birds fly?

Another way to make a question is to split a compound verb and put part before the subject. *For example:*

Can birds fly?
Do birds fly?

Sentence combining

Sometimes sentences can be improved by combining two short sentences into one longer sentence. *For example:*

Boys go to school.   +   Girls go to school.
Boys and girls go to school.

Sentence untangling

Sometimes sentences get hopelessly long or tangled up. While technically they are correct sentences, they can be made more understandable by dividing them into two or more sentences. *For example:*

After losing almost all the games during the season, the school that the boys went to won the big basketball game last year.

The boy's school won the big basketball game last year. They lost most of the other games during the season.

Beginning writers sometimes make awkward sentences by using too many "and's". These are called "run on" sentences. They can be improved by breaking them into two or more sentences. *For example:*

I went home and I saw my dog and I gave him something to eat and I played with him.

When I went home I saw my dog. I gave him something to eat. Then I played with him.

Prepositional Phrases

A prepositional phrase is simply two or more words beginning with a preposition and which does not contain both a subject and a verb. A prepositional phrase can be added to a sentence in several places. In the following sentences we will illustrate how the prepositional phrase "at night" can be put in different parts of the sentence:

Birds fly home at night.
At night, birds fly home.
Birds, at night, fly home.

The first sentence is probably the best sentence because if flows better. The second sentence is a little awkward, but maybe the writer wishes to stress the "night" part of the message. The third sentence might be correct grammar but it is indeed awkward and doesn't sound good because it puts distance between the subject and the verb.

Clauses

A clause is a group of words that does contain a subject (noun or pronoun) and a predicate (verb) that can be added to a sentence. *For example:*

He took a bath <u>before he ate dinner.</u>

The "before he ate dinner" is a <u>dependent clause</u> and it can't stand alone like a sentence because the "before" puts in a condition that must be satisfied. The "He took a bath" is an <u>independent clause</u>. It could stand alone if the writer wanted to shorten the sentence.

Paragraphs

There aren't many real rules about paragraphs. They can be any length, but modern writers prefer short paragraphs. Even one sentence paragraphs are O.K.

However, you must indent at the beginning of each paragraph.

In writing dialogue, you must have a new paragraph every time you change speakers.

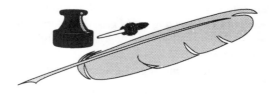

SENTENCES - ADVANCED CONSTRUCTION

1. Vary sentence length

Good writers use a combination of long and short sentences. For example:

Short sentences have punch. Long involved sentences sometimes are necessary but often they are harder to read and leave the reader rather confused.

2. Vary word order

The typical sentence is called a "declarative sentence" and it uses the order subject-verb-object. For example: *Birds fly home after dark.*

You can add variety by

a. starting with a verb phrase. For example:

Flying home after dark is what some birds like.

To fly home is important for some birds.

3. Use the active voice

The active voice is easier to read and uses less words. For example:

John read the book. (active voice)

The book was read by John. (passive voice)

Rattlesnakes should not be stepped on. (passive voice)

Don't step on rattlesnakes. (active voice)

There are times when you want to use the passive in order to emphasize something. For example, if you wish to emphasize the "football game" instead of "canceling", you might use the following passive sentence:

The football game was canceled because of rain.

4. Avoid negative sentences

It is better to state something positively. Watch out for the word "not".

John did not tell the truth. (negative)

John told a lie. (positive)

5. Be concrete

Use concrete examples and descriptions. Something concrete is something you can see, feel, hear, or touch.

The crowd was noisy. (abstract)

The crowd was yelling and screaming. (concrete)

He was a big man. (abstract)

He was nearly 7 feet tall. (concrete)

87

BUILD A SENTENCE
Select one from each column

Who? (Subject)	What? (Verb)	Why? (prep phrase)	When? (adverb)	Where? (object)
A boy	climbed into an airplane	for a vacation	last summer	in New York
				on the moon
The shark	looked everywhere	to find his mother	in 2020	outside my house
A big dump truck	slid	to get a million dollars	during the game	in a cave
The Monster	laughed			on a farm
	swam	for fun	next year	
My Dad	dove			under a rock
			today	
A rattlesnake	swung on a rope	because he was on fire	at midnight	next to a lion
				100 feet beneath the ocean
Maria	fell	to fall in love	forever	
Mickey Mouse		for an ice cream cone	before breakfast	in bed
	yelled loudly			on top of a tree
A tiny ant	flew	to build a house	always	
				at the circus
The train	ran fast	to fight the enemy	500 years ago	in front of the city hall
Iron John	jumped			
		to get to school	right now	in a corn field
A beautiful princess	kicked			
	couldn't stop	to be kissed	in a month	behind the stove
A large bird	slithered	for a coat of paint	after school	in space
My good friend				downtown
	crawled	because it was mad	in an hour	
				inside an egg
A teacher	hopped on one foot			
			yesterday	in Africa
			during the war	out West
			at dawn	on a tropical island

Feel free to add more words to make your sentence read better or add interest. You can leave out anything except a subject and a verb.

VERB ERRORS

Oh, we hate to open up a discussion of verbs. It is like opening up a can of worms.

Native speakers of a language learn most verb grammar rules by simple usage. If their parents speak good English, for example, then usually the children will just grow up speaking good (standard) English. That's the easy way to learn grammar.

However, it doesn't always work. Some households do not speak standard English, at least not all the time. Some households don't even speak English and the student must learn it in school, on the playground, or in the workplace.

There is another problem and that is written English is more formal than spoken English. When we write, we must use sentences, and verbs must be used correctly.

Error Number 1 (transitive/intransitive verb use)

It is correct to write a simple sentence of just a subject (noun or pronoun) and a predicate (verb) such as: "Birds fly." But you can't have a simple sentence like: "Birds flew" or "The farmer milked"

Why not? Because there are two kinds of verbs. One kind of verb, called intransitive, does not require an object, for example "Birds fly". But the other kind, called transitive, must have an object, for example "The birds flew south" or "The farmer milked his cow".

There is a special kind of transitive verb, called a linking verb, in which the word or words following the verb are not really an object but rather they refer back to the subject. For example: "His load was heavy".

In case you would like to simplify all this, let's just say:
"Watch out, some verbs must have something after them".

Error Number 2 (person/number verb use)

You can't say: "He walk home." or "He be home."
Why not? Because verbs have to agree with the subject in terms of "person" and "number".

In English there are three persons, I, you, and he/she, and two numbers, single and plural. Here is a table of person and number for a regular verb:

	Singular	**Plural**
1st person	I walk	we walk
2nd person	you walk	you walk
3rd person	he/she walks	they walk

Note that the only change in the verb "walk" is in the 3rd person singular where "walk" becomes "walks". Most English verbs follow this pattern of adding "s" (or "es"- see spelling rules) to the verb whenever you use the 3rd person singular.

Hence, you can't say "He walk home" because the third person singular requires that you use "walks" and "He walks home" is correct.

However, there is one verb that we use all the time, which is not regular at all, and that is the verb "to be". It looks like this:

	Singular	**Plural**
1st person	I am	we are
2nd person	you are	you are
3rd person	he/she is	they are

Hence, the form for the verb "to be" in the 3rd person singular is "is" and "He is home" is correct. One American dialect, Black English, might use "He be home" sometimes in speaking, and if you are writing dialect in a story it is o.k. to use it inside quotation marks.

Error Number 3   (tense - past)

You can't say "He walks yesterday" or "He is home yesterday". Why not? Because verbs have a present tense (time) and a past tense, and yesterday is already past so you have to use a past verb. Hence you have to say: "He walked yesterday" or "He was home yesterday".
Here are the present and past tenses for a regular verb like "walk" and the verb "to be".

	Regular Verb		**Verb "to be"**	
	Present	Past	Present	Past
(Singular)				
1st person - I walk	walked	am	was	
2nd person - you walk	walked	are	were	
3rd person - he walks	walked	is	was	
(Plural)				
1st person - we walk	walked	are	were	
2nd person - you walk	walked	are	were	
3rd person - they walk	walked	are	were	

Error Number 4 (tense - future)

You can't say: "I walk tomorrow" or "I am home tomorrow"
Why not? Because you have to use the future tense.

To form the future tense for a regular verb is very easy – just add "will" in front of the present tense. Thus, "I will walk tomorrow" is correct.

To form the future tense for the verb "to be" is a little different. You use "will be" for all persons, singular and plural. Thus, "I will be home tomorrow" is correct.

Most of the time in your writing you will use either the present, the past, or the future tense. But we might as well tell you about two more possible errors.

Error Number 5 (present participle)

You can't say: "He is walk home". Why not? Because when you use the present tense of the verb "to be" in front of a verb, you have to use the present participle form of the verb.

Fortunately this is very simple because most present participles are formed by simply adding "ing". Hence, "He is walking home" is correct.

Error Number 6 (past participle)

You can't say: "I have walk yesterday". Why not? Because when you put "have", "has", or "had" in front of the verb you need the past participle form. The past participle form for regular verbs is easy, it is just like the past. In other words, you just add "ed" to the verb if it is a regular verb. Hence, "I have walked yesterday" is correct.

One serious little difficulty with past participles is that some of them, not many, but some, are irregular. For example, you can't say, "I have flyed before" because "fly" has an irregular participle. You must say, "I have flown before".

So some verbs are irregular in the past tense or in the past participle.

See the next page for some common irregular verbs.

Error Number 7 (boredom)

Make your writing interesting by using exciting or unusual verbs.

Don't say, "He hit the ball".

Say, "He smashed the ball".

Or say, "He whammed the ball".

VERBS - IRREGULAR

Most verbs are regular. This usually means that to change from the present to the past you simply add the suffix "-ed". For example: "walk - walked". But some verbs are irregular and that means that the past and/or participle are different. See the Spelling Rules for more discussion of verbs.

Present	**Past**	**Past Participle**
am	was	been
are	were	been
bite	bit	bitten
catch	caught	caught
dive	dove	dived
drink	drank	drunk
do	did	done
fly	flew	flown
give	gave	given
go	went	gone
know	knew	known
put	put	put
ring	rang	rung
see	saw	seen
sing	sang	sung
steal	stole	stolen
swim	swam	swum
take	took	taken
wear	wore	worn
write	wrote	written

Just in case you would like to see how irregular verbs can be, here is a little summary of most of the kinds of irregular verb changes:

	Infinitive & Present	**Past**	**Past Participle**
a. some change all forms	give	gave	given
b. some never change	hit	hit	hit
c. some have the same past & past participle hold	held	held
d. a few change past only	run	ran	run

PARTS OF SPEECH

It is sometimes helpful to understand grammar if you know about Parts of Speech, which is a way of classifying words. Look over these 8 basic classes of words, then read the caution at the end and this is most of what beginning writers need to know.

NOUN: The name of a person, place or thing. A simple test for a noun is if you can put the word "the" or "a" in front of it, it is probably a noun.

Ex: ball, hat, dog, man

Proper nouns are names of a particular person, place or thing. The importance of knowing about proper nouns is that you must capitalize them every time you use them.

Ex: Mr. Smith, America, Fido

Every sentence must have a noun or pronoun.

(See Capitalization section on page 74)

PRONOUN: A word used in place of a noun.

Ex: he, you, it, their, someone

ADJECTIVE: A word that describes a noun or pronoun.

Ex: green, big, all, those, some

Note there is a special kind of an adjective called an **Article** and there are only 3 articles, "the", "a", and "an".

VERB: A word that shows some kind of action or state.

Ex: run, study, read, is

Every sentence must have a verb.

ADVERB: A word that describes a verb.

Ex: quietly, fearfully, very, often, too

CONJUNCTION: A word used to join words or phrases.

Ex: and, or, but, because

PREPOSITION: A word used to show relationship of a noun or pronoun to another word. This is a little hard to understand, but if you think of a preposition as being put in front of a noun (forming a prepositional phrase), then that prepositional phrase acts like an adjective or adverb. In other words, the prepositional phrase can modify the noun or pronoun, or a prepositional phrase can modify a verb.

Examples of prepositions: of, from, above, at. to, with

Prepositional phrase examples: Bill, from Arkansas, was the first choice.

Bill hit the ball to Jose .

INTERJECTION: A word that expresses strong emotion.
Ex: Darn! Help! Oh!

Caution: The same word can be used as different parts of speech. The real determiner is how the word is used in a sentence.

Ex: This is a <u>light</u> box. (adjective)
The <u>light</u> is broken.(noun)
Please <u>light</u> the lamp. (verb)

He drives <u>fast</u>. (adverb)
He is a <u>fast</u> driver. (adjective)
The <u>fast</u> is over. (noun)

Here is a helpful hint: If you can put an article like "the" in front of a word, it is a noun. *Ex:* "the box". But you can have an adjective between the noun and the article. *Ex:* "the big box". Also remember adjectives modify nouns, and adverbs modify verbs, and adverbs.

COMPARATIVE ADJECTIVES

Adjectives (words which modify nouns) come in three degrees:

Positive	Comparative	Superlative
Most adjectives are **regular** and look like this:		
high	higher ("er" added)	highest ("est" added)

But some adjectives are irregular and look like this:

good	better	best
bad	worse	worst
many	more	most
little	less	least

However, many two or more syllable adjectives form the Comparative and Superlative by adding more/most or less/least. For example:

beautiful	more beautiful	most beautiful
famous	less famous	least famous
(or going the other way)		
famous	more famous	most famous

TYPES AND USES OF WRITING

WRITING USES

There are many uses for writing. Here is a list of some common ones. Use this list as a suggestion for practicing different writing uses.

Stories

humorous - serious
short - long
mystery - adventure
family - travel
fiction - nonfiction; fact - fantasy - opinion

Autobiography

of me

Biography

of my mother, friend, relative, the teacher

Poems

about friend, death, home, farm, mountain, lake; (rhyme - nonrhyme)

Letter

to grandparent, friend, Santa Claus, the President of U.S. (business - personal - short note)

Directions

to my house, how to skate, care for a bike, feed a pet

Invitation

to a birthday, for a dinner, to spend a weekend

Newspaper article

news, sports, book review, TV review, movie review, play review

Report

for science, for social studies

THANK YOU NOTE OR FRIENDLY LETTER FORM

When you receive a gift or someone does you a favor, you write a thank you note. Usually, it is short and follows the form of a friendly letter.

HEADING	*167 George Road* *Columbus, NJ 08022* *January 12, 1993*
GREETING	*Dear Aunt June,*
BODY	*Thank you for the green gift. You are right. It is my favorite color! Yesterday, I went to the mall and bought some video tapes. Next time you come over, I'll show them to you and thank you in person.*
CLOSING	*Your nephew,*
SIGNATURE	*Zach*

A thank you note starts with a <u>heading</u> that states your address and the date. Be sure to put a comma between the city and state and between the day of the month and the year.

The first word of the <u>greeting</u> is usually "Dear." Notice it begins with a capital letter. The second word of the greeting is the name of the person receiving the letter, and it is followed by a comma.

The part of the note where you say thank you is called the <u>body</u>. In a friendly letter, this is where you write your news or message. The first word of every paragraph is indented.

The <u>closing</u> shows who wrote the note. Notice that only the first word is capitalized, and a comma follows the last word. The closing lines up with the heading and <u>signature</u>, which is your name.

BUSINESS LETTER FORM

When you wish to order something through the mail, ask for permission, or get some information, you write a business letter. It is different from a friendly letter. There is an inside address and the punctuation after the greeting is not the same.

320 20th Avenue Menomonie, WI 54751 January 14, 1993	*HEADING*
Ms. Heather Kistler, Director Arkansas Department of Tourism Box 1107 Little Rock, Arkansas 72201	*INSIDE* *ADDRESS*
Dear Ms. Kistler:	*GREETING*
My family is planning on taking a camping trip this summer. Please send me a state map and some information about campgrounds and what places to see. Right now we are interested in the Hot Springs National Park area. Information about other interesting parts of the state will help us decide what else to visit.	*BODY*
Yours truly,	*CLOSING*
Kara Zola	*SIGNATURE*

A business letter starts with a <u>heading</u>. It gives your address and the date. Notice that there is a comma between the city and state and between the day of the month and the year.

The <u>inside address</u> gives the name, title, and address of the person to whom you are writing as well as the name of the company. Don't forget to put a comma between the person's name and title and be sure to capitalize the title.

The <u>greeting</u> is followed by a colon (:) in a business letter. Then comes the body or content of the letter.

In the <u>closing</u>, only the first word is capitalized. In a business letter, you can close with "Respectfully," "Sincerely," or "Yours truly." Only the first word is capitalized, and a comma follows the second word.

The closing and the <u>signature</u>, which is the writer's name, line up with the closing.

Add your position after the signature if it is appropriate.
For example: Joe Smith
            Asst. Manager

Add enclosures if any at the bottom after the signature.
For example: Enclosed, 2 photographs.

BOOK REPORT FORM

In a book report, tell what a book is about and also give your opinion of it. The form below will help you.

Title (Underline and capitalize all important words.)

Author

(What is the book about? Who? What? Where? When? Why? How?)

_____

_____

_____

_____

_____

_____

(Who is your favorite or least favorite character? Why? When?)

_____

_____

_____

(What is your opinion of the book? Why? At what part?)

_____

_____

_____

(Do you recommend this book? If so, to whom? Why?)

_____

_____

_____

STORY SUMMARIZING FORM

Often you are asked to retell or summarize a story. The following form shows all the parts of a story. It is called a story map. If you write about each story part, your summary will be complete.

When you are writing a story, you can use this same form to help you plan what you want to say.

STORY MAP

Title: _____

Characters: _____
(Main character and/or other major characters)
_____

_____

Setting: _____
_____

_____

Problem: _____
_____

_____

Events: _____
(or plan)

   1. _____

   2. _____

   3. _____

Outcome: _____
(or result)
_____

KEEPING A DAILY JOURNAL

A daily journal is like a diary. The difference is that you don't write anything secret or private in it, the way you might in a diary. Many writers view the journal as their best friend. It's a place where you can:

- jot down an idea

- experiment with writing

- write a creative story or poem

- expand your vocabulary by writing down new words you like

- practice writing every day

- record an impression of the weather

- write how you feel at a particular time

- tell your reaction to what is happening around you

- write down an opinion of a book, a movie, or music

Your recorded thoughts can serve as a source of ideas for writing at a later time. Often you will write about things in your journal that you will want to share with others.

Tips for Writing in Your Journal

1. Date each entry.

2. Begin by writing three to five minutes a day. Move up gradually to 10 minutes a day.

3. Write when you feel relaxed, if possible.

4. Don't worry about spelling or punctuation. The important thing is that you are writing and getting ideas down on paper.

5. If doing creative writing, you could use one of the ideas on the "Things to Write in Your Journal" list, or you might like to use a "story starter." See page 113 for some more ideas.

6. Write in complete sentences when you put down your thoughts.

7. Use action verbs and the present tense to keep your writing lively.

8. Use adjectives and adverbs to give a clearer picture.

Things to Write About in Your Journal

1. Write about your hobby or something you would like to do as a hobby.

2. Tell about the history of your state or your town.

3. What is the best thing about living today? The worst thing?

4. What pictures come to your mind when you think about nature?

5. Write a poem about a sunrise, a sunset, or anything that interests you.

6. Find a picture that you like. React to it in your journal.

7. Write about something you have just learned about.

8. Tell how schools today are different from when your grandparents went to school.

9. Describe your favorite quiet place. Tell what you think about when you are there.

10. Write about a beach or lake shore near where you live. What have you found when you have combed the beach?

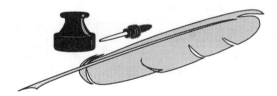

GRAPH TYPES

The purpose of this list is to show some of the varieties of graphical expression used by writers. Good writers use a lot of graphs and illustrations. Good graphs make the writing more meaningful.

1. Lineal

a. Simple   story

b. Multiple   history

c. Complex

    Hierarchy   organization

    Flow   computer

    Process   chemicals

    Sociogram   friendship

2. Quantitative

a. Frequency Polygon   growth

b. Bar Graph   comparisons

c. Scattergram   test scores

d. Spread Sheet   scheduling

e. Pie Graph   percentage

f. Dials   clock

From "Graphical Literacy" by Edward Fry, Journal of Reading Feb. 1991. Also see "Theory of Graphs" Eric #ED 240 528

3. Spatial

a. Two Dimensional
(single plane)   map   floor plan

b. Three Dimensional
(multiplane)   relief map    math shapes

4. Pictorial

a. Realistic

b. Semipictorial

c. Abstract

5. Hypothetical

 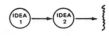

a. Conceptual

b. Verbal

6. Near Graphs

a. High Verbal Outline Main Idea
         a. Detail
         b. Another Detail

b. High Numerical

TABLE	
25	4.2
37	6.1
21	7.3

c. Symbols $ ✠ 🚭

d. Decorative Design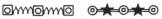

103

TIPS ON IMPROVING
YOUR VOCABULARY

Writers notice and collect words. The following are some tips that will help you make your vocabulary larger and more interesting.

1. Start a word bank. Decorate a coffee can, a small box, or an envelope. Also cut some 3" by 5" index cards into smaller word cards. Whenever you come across a word that interests you, write it on a small word card and put it in the word bank. You might want to write the meaning of the word on the back of the card along with a sentence using the word.

2. Nouns help you create word pictures. Look around you. What nouns do you notice? Write the less common ones on small word cards and put them in your word bank.

3. Some nouns name certain groups of things. They are called collective nouns. Use them where they fit. Some examples are: "colony of ants," "crowd of people," "fleet of taxicabs," "flock of sheep," "gaggle of geese," "herd of cattle," "pride of lions," and "swarm of mosquitos." Do you know anymore? Add whatever new ones you find to your word bank.

4. Action verbs tell what happens to the subject. Look in your journal and list 10 action verbs. Trade your list with a partner. Each use the other's action verbs in sentences.

5. Some words echo the sounds they name, such as "buzz," "crash," "flop," and "zoom." Listen to the sounds around you. Make a list of other words that sound like the things they name. Add them to your word bank.

6. Trade papers with a classmate. Find his or her adjectives and/or adverbs. Add the ones that interest you to your word bank.

7. Reread the last thing you wrote. List the verbs, nouns, pronouns, adverbs, adjectives, and conjunctions in separate columns. If you notice any interesting or unusual words, add them to your word bank.

THE WRITING PROCESS

No doubt, you do a lot of writing. Sometimes you write for other people, such as a note to a friend. Sometimes you write for yourself, perhaps in a daily journal or just a note to remind yourself about something you have to do. Probably you often write quickly, without giving the words or the order of the ideas too much thought.

Then there are times when you want to write something good enough to share with other people. That is a good time to use the writing process step by step. There are four stages: prewriting, writing, revising, and proofreading.

Few people write well on the first try. It takes time. Time is needed to think, to plan, to gather ideas (stage one, prewriting). After you have written (stage two, writing), you need more time to review it. Then time is needed for changes (stage three, revising) and for corrections (stage four, proofreading). Some ideas that will help while you are in each of the four stages are given on the pages that follow.

STAGE 1 - PREWRITING
GET READY TO WRITE

Most writers don't know what they want to say before they begin. You need to take time to get ideas. Here are some things that you can try:

1. **Brainstorm** by yourself or with a partner or several others.
2. Write an important word or idea on a page and draw a circle around it. Then cluster other related words on the same page. By the time you have finished filling up the paper with other words that go with the word in the circle or with the original idea, you will have many thoughts to write about. This is called **clustering.**
3. Fold a paper into four **sections.** Then write a thought that goes with the thing or topic you are writing about. After you have filled in each section, go back and put a number on each part. Put a one before the idea you should write about first, then a two before the next idea in order. If you used both sides of the sheet, you will number up to eight. Many students do this when they answer essay questions on tests.
4. **Interview** someone. It might be a parent, a teacher, a student, or someone in the community. Prepare a list of questions in advance. When the person you interview answers your questions, he or she will trigger some additional thoughts in your head on the thing or topic you are to write about. Talking to someone else usually helps you prepare to write. Often two heads really are better than one.

5. Keep a **journal.** Carry one with you when you are working on a writing project. Jot down ideas when they come into your mind. If you happen to see something that relates to your writing topic, record your impressions right away. Try to write in the journal everyday. It might be an idea, an opinion, or an impression. When you have to come up with an original idea for something to write about, you probably will be able to find a topic here. Also, keeping a journal will provide you with practice in expressing yourself with words. It will give you a chance to experiment with writing. See pages 113 - 116 for some story ideas.

STAGE 2 - WRITING
PUT YOUR IDEAS ON PAPER

Now that you have gone through the prewriting stage, you have a topic to write about and some notes. That's a good start, but what do you do about that empty piece of paper in front of you? That's easy – just start writing! Now is the time to get your ideas down on paper. All the words probably won't be spelled right. Some of your ideas will be out of order. In the revising and proofreading stages you will improve what you have written and correct any mistakes. It is a good idea to write only on every other line so that you will have plenty of room to make changes later.

Try one of the following ideas to get you started or help you continue to write:
1. Write a title or a phrase for the topic you are writing about on a sheet of paper. Then list the first 10 words that pop into your mind. Choose any three words of those 10, and use them in your first sentence. Finally expand that sentence by explaining it throughout the rest of the paragraph. If your topic were "Buying a Gift," you might quickly list "bathrobe," "purple," "department store," "mortician," "long," "pole," "steps," "crumpled," "sadly," and "broken." The three you select might be "bathrobe," "department store," and "mortician." When you create the topic sentence, you might come up with:

> The town's mortician went into its largest department store looking for a bathrobe. At first, the salesclerk who waited on him thought that nothing was unusual. But after showing Mr. Dragonne every bathrobe in stock, she began to feel uneasy. Why didn't he leave? Why didn't he go to another store? Or why didn't he ask her to order one that she had in a different size? Mr. Dragonne seemed to be taking his time. He talked very slowly, and he moved very slowly. The salesclerk became more and more nervous.

If you cannot think of what to write for the second paragraph, select a word or idea related to the first paragraph you have just written. List ten more words very quickly, without thinking. Pick three of them, and write the first sentence of the second paragraph. Then write more about that first sentence to complete the second paragraph.

2. Ask a **question** at the beginning of your writing. During the prewriting stage, you may have observed something carefully, perhaps a dog scratching himself, and made notes on it. Read over your notes and come up with a question that you can begin your writing with, such as "Did you ever notice how a dog scratches himself?" Then use your notes to describe what happens. You may not have to use all the notes you took. Just use the best details that you noted. Finally, add an "ending sentence," such as "We should have named him Itchy!"

3. Begin by making a **statement about a character**. For example, you could say, "There was a big bully with bright red hair who liked to chase his classmates home from school."

4. Begin by having the **main character speak**. For example, you might write, "'Ha! Scared you again! I love to chase scaredy cats,' said the red haired bully."

5. Open with **your opinion**. Write it as though you were talking to a friend. You could begin with a sentence like this: "David, some day you should try to be pleasant to your classmates. Have you ever thought about sharing the dessert your mother packs in your lunch each day?"

6. Start with **a simile**. Compare unlike things using the words "like" or "as." You might write: "The school stands like a fort." "His hair was as bright as a stop light." See pages 117 - 121 for additional writing techniques.

7. When you don't know where to begin or what to say next, you have what is called writer's block. One way to break the block is to **write your name over and over**. Do that until an idea pops into your mind. You'll be surprised at how quickly another idea will come when you keep your writing hand moving.

8. Another way to break a writer's block is to **rearrange** what you have already written. Often the place were you are stuck is not really the problem. You may have made a wrong turn a few paragraphs back, and now you are at a dead end. The only way out of a dead end is to go back to the place where you made the wrong turn. By rearranging what you are writing, you can find the place that is causing trouble.

9. Writing **does not have to be done in order**, from beginning to end. Sometimes it is easier to write the end or the middle before the beginning. Begin wherever you can. You can always rearrange later.

STAGE 3 - REVISING
IMPROVE YOUR WRITING BY MAKING CHANGES

Reading to yourself is an important step in revising. Ask yourself if you have met your purpose. Think about the audience. Will they understand your message? You will probably need to cross out some words and write in new ones. Maybe you will want to draw arrows to show where words or sentences should be moved. Revisions are often done in another color pencil or ink. Don't worry about your writing looking messy at this point. You will make it look neat again later.

Next, read what you have written to a partner. Ask him or her what part was best and was there anything he or she would like to know more about. Ask if the sequential order is correct. Find out if your partner can offer any suggestions. Then make more changes, if you think they will improve what you have written.

Compare what you have written to the revision checklist.

<u>Revision Checklist</u>

_____   **1. Did I meet my purpose? Some possibilities are listed:**

____ Did I write about something that happened to me?

____ Did I tell about something I can do?

____ Did I try to persuade someone to try something?

____ Did I try to persuade someone to buy something?

____ Did I get across my vision of something?

____ Did I explain how to do something?

____ Did I write a biography of a real person?

____ Did I write a description of something?

____ Did I write a fairy tale, fable or fantasy?

____ Did I write a humorous story?

____ Did I compare two things?

____ Did I write a poem?

____ Did I describe something, like my favorite food?

____ Other

_____   **2. Will my audience respond to what I have written?**

____ Will they understand?

____ Will they enjoy it?

____ Will they be persuaded?

____ Will they be able to follow the steps?

_____ 3. Is what I have written in order?

_____ 4. Did I include interesting facts and facts that readers would like to know (if appropriate)?

_____ 5. Did I give facts and reasons to support my opinion (if appropriate)?

_____ 6. If I wrote about two things, did I tell how they are alike?

_____ 7. If I wrote about two things, did I tell how they are different?

_____ 8. If I wrote about two things, did I use any similes or metaphors?

_____ 9. Are there more exact or stronger words that I could use? (A thesaurus is a good place for finding other words with similar meanings.)

_____ 10. Did I overuse any words? (Look in a thesaurus to find more interesting words.)

_____ 11. Did I put too many ideas in one sentence? Can I improve a sentence by making two or more shorter sentences?

_____ 12. Did I keep my sentences short enough? (Usually, the shorter the sentence the easier it is to read.)

_____ 13. Did I avoid using too many short sentences so that my writing doesn't sound choppy?

_____ 14. Did I use different kinds of sentences, such as exclamatory or interrogatory, to make my writing interesting?

_____ 15. Did I use positive words? (Positive sentences are easier to understand than negative ones.) Not this: We can't go until Monday. But this: We can go Monday.

_____ 16. Have I used the same nouns and verbs too often? Can I replace a repeated word with one that means the same?

_____ 17. Can I replace some nouns with pronouns to add variety?

_____ 18. Are some sentences fuzzy? (If you replace too many nouns with pronouns, some sentences will become unclear.)

_____ 19. Did I use "I" and "me" correctly?

_____ 20. Do the verbs agree with the subjects of the sentences?

_____ 21. Was I careful when forming the past tense of irregular verbs?

_____ 22. Are all the verbs in the same tense (the same time)?

_____ 23. Did I overuse common adjectives, such as "good," "bad," and "nice?"

_____ 24. Do adjectives add details and help form sharp word pictures?

_____ 25. Did I use adverbs to give information about "how," "when," and "where" and to make my meaning more clear?

_____ 26. Was I careful not to start any sentences with the conjunctions "and" or "but"?

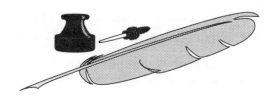

STAGE 4 - PROOFREADING
FIND AND FIX THE ERRORS

Now that you have checked to see that what you have written says what you want it to say, it is time to proofread it. By proofreading, you are being polite. You are making it easier for the reader to read and understand what you have written.

Look for only one type of error at a time. For example, you might look for spelling errors first. Later you can look for other kinds of errors in capitalizing, punctuating, and indenting.

When proofreading, it is a good idea to put a sheet of paper or a ruler under each line as you read it. That way you will be more likely to find any mistakes. It is easier to find spelling errors if you read each line backward or read only every other word and then go back to check the words you skipped. That way you think about each word separately instead of the meaning of the whole sentence or paragraph.

Perhaps you can find someone to read what you have written. It is usually easier to spot someone else's mistakes. Maybe you can read the other person's work and help each other fix mistakes. When proofreading someone else's writing, put a circle around any errors.

When you find a error in your own writing, use a proofreading mark. Often the color red is used so that the marks will stand out. There is a list of proofreading marks on page 112.

The proofreading checklist will help you to find your errors.

Proofreading Checklist

_____ 1. **Did I spell words correctly?** (Use the Spelling Checker on pp. 9 - 66)

_____ 2. **Did I capitalize correctly?** (See page 74)

_____ 3. **Did I indent each paragraph?**

_____ 4. **Did I use the correct punctuation mark at the end of each sentence?**

_____ 5. **Did I put commas in the right places?** (See page 77)

_____ 6. **Did I use clear, readable handwriting?**

_____ 7. **Did I dot every "i" and cross every "t"?**

_____ 8. **Did I leave the right amount of space between each word so that the words aren't crowded?**

_____ 9. **Did I space the letters so that each can be clearly seen?**

_____ 10. **Is there a little extra space between each sentence?**

_____ 11. **Does every sentence have a noun and a verb?**

Sharing

Often writers have trouble seeing their own mistakes. Let someone else proofread your writing. After proofreading, give what you have written an interesting title, copy it very neatly and share it with others. You could read it aloud to them. You might record it on an audio tape and play it for someone. Or maybe you'd like to put your writing on a bulletin board for many people to see and enjoy. An important part of writing is getting a response from an audience, so share what you have written!

PROOFREADING SYMBOLS

Teachers and editors often use these symbols to tell the writer or typist how to correct errors or improve the writing.

Notation in Margin	How Indicated in Copy	Explanation
¶	true. ∧The best rule to follow	New Paragraph
⌒	living room	Close up
#	Mary had∧a	Insert Space
⁀	Mary had a lamb little	Transpose
sp	There were ⑤ children	Spell out
cap	mary had a little lamb	Capitalize
lc	Mary had a little /amb	Lower case
e	The correct proce/dure	Delete or take out
stet	Mary had a little lamb	Restore crossed-out word (s)
little	Mary had a∧lamb	Insert word (s) in margin
⊙	Birds fly∧	Insert a period
∧	Next∧the main	Insert a comma

STORY STARTERS

INTERESTING TITLES

The Me That Nobody Knows

The Super-duper Market

The Tallest Tale of All

The Farm in the City

My Best Quality

The Lost Suitcase

The Perfect Gift

The Sleepless Night

The Turquoise Airplane

The Day Without Sunshine

The Elephant Without Ears

The Circus Came to Town

The Giraffe Without a Neck

The Troll Under the Bridge

The Machine That Came Alive

The Visitor at Midnight

The Big Wish

Vitamin Soup

The Sleeping Guard

The Disappearing Backpack

The Big White Lie

The Web

The Giant Shrimp

The Whimpering Puppy

In the Dark

The Wacky Weekend

OPENING SENTENCES

- I won't be attending school for the rest of the year because . . .
- My favorite childhood toy was . . .
- My favorite teacher is . . . because . . .
- If I could be any animal in the zoo, I would be . . .
- I gave a classmate some garlic flavored chewing gum because . . .
- The best day of my life was when . . .
- The worst day of my life was when . . .
- If I could be anybody, I'd like to be . . .
- If I were invited to write for a television show, I'd write scripts for . . .
- When I raise children, I'll never . . .
- Ten (or as many as you can think of) uses for a pillow case are . . .
- The thunder and lightning frightened me so much that I . . .
- The nonsense word "nooeaia" means . . .
- A blue monster got on the bus and . . .
- I had a nightmare about . . .
- My goal in life is to . . .
- I just bought a new . . .
- My favorite time of day is . . .
- When the sun came up, I . . .
- My favorite song makes me feel . . .
- I like the (your favorite) music group because . . .
- If I were a teacher, I would . . .
- The flowers suddenly bloomed when . . .
- When the door burst open, . . .
- My favorite possession is . . .
- My favorite author is . . .
- My favorite book is . . .
- The most exciting thing that ever happened at school was . . .
- The last movie I saw was . . .
- My favorite comic strip character is . . .
- I would like to be . . .
- Holidays (or name a specific holiday) make (s) me feel . . .
- I can hardly wait to . . .

GREAT QUESTIONS

- Where do lost socks and gloves go?
- What piece of furniture am I most like? Why?
- Who would I like to look like? Why? What would I do differently if I looked like that person?
- What character in a book would you like to meet? Why?
- What will you be when you are an adult?
- What century would you like to live in?
- If you couldn't live on earth, what planet would you go to? Why?
- What words have you invented? Why? What do they mean?
- Did you ever take a plane trip by yourself? Where? Why?
- What is it like sitting next to you in the school cafeteria?
- What do you think the class president will be doing in twenty years?
- Why do you like to talk on the phone to your best friend?
- If you could change you house, what would it be like?
- What might happen today that would make you very happy or very sad?
- What is an average day in your life like?
- Where would you rather live?
- What does the moon think about the sun?
- What do the clouds think about the airplanes?
- Why do the stars twinkle so brightly?
- What was your favorite fairy tale? Why?
- What is your favorite cartoon? Why?
- Why has the hair on only one side of your head been cut off?
- If you could trade anything you have, what would it be? Why?
- What would you do if you were a giant?
- How would one of your parents describe you?
- If you were a teacher, how would you handle a student who misbehaves?
- What is your favorite after-school activity?
- What would you do if you were served purple spinach?
- What would you do today if you could do anything you wanted?
- How do you care for the classroom pet?
- What would you pack for a trip to Disney World?
- What commercial don't you like? Why?
- What new skill have you learned lately (riding a bike, batting a ball)? What was difficult about it and in what order did you learn?

STORY ENDERS

I have never in my life been more frightened.

We had to buy it even though we really didn't want it anymore.

That finally persuaded me to give up chocolate.

Then they charged me five dollars.

That is a day I'd like to forget.

It was a day I'll always remember.

Now it is a common saying among my friends (or family).

This event has changed my life forever.

Now he/she is my favorite hero/heroine.

That's the last time I'll ever play hide and seek.

It cost a lot of money, but it was worth it.

It was the right choice.

Obviously, I made the wrong choice.

Then the lights went out.

That's why they named the town Cleverville.

Now my friends say I could be a cartoon hero/heroine.

Everything he had said was an exaggeration.

To this day, I won't eat that food.

It was the best smell in the world.

Now you can understand why I was so mad.

That was the end of a perfect week.

We'll never go back there again.

Even though I felt tired, it was a job well done.

They don't think of me as just a kid anymore.

It was the worst vacation we ever had.

Finally, we had to let it go.

CONTRACTIONS

Contractions are combinations of two words to make a shorter form.

am
I'm

is, has
he's
she's
it's
what's

would, had
I'd
you'd
he'd
she'd
we'd
they'd
it'd
there'd
what'd
who'd

not
can't
don't
isn't
won't
shouldn't
couldn't
wouldn't
aren't
doesn't
wasn't
weren't
hasn't
haven't
hadn't

are
you're
we're
they're
who're

us
let's

have
I've
you've
we've
they've
could've
would've
should've
might've
who've
there've

will
I'll
you'll
she'll
he'll
it'll
we'll
they'll
that'll
these'll
those'll
there'll
this'll
what'll
who'll

JAZZ UP YOUR WRITING STYLE
(Literary Terms)

The following contains a list of literary terms and descriptions of elements of writing and variations of writing. Look them over. They can add a new element or a bit of sparkle to your writing. They might suggest something you never use but ought to, at least on occasion.

Alliteration. Alliteration occurs when two or more words have the same beginning sound. *Example: Mike mixed some malt in his milk.*

Antithesis. Contrasting words or ideas by asserting something and denying its contrary or by parallel or balanced phrases. *Example: This soup should be eaten cold, not hot.*

Antonym. The opposite of a synonym is called an antonym. This is a word that means the opposite or near the opposite. For example, "come - go" and "up - down" are antonyms. You can sometimes improve your writing by putting in an antonym for emphasis. *Examples: "I mean up, not down." "Mother didn't ask him to work, she told him to work."* Here are a few antonyms:

large - small	**top - bottom**
then - now	**clean - dirty**
first - last	**good - bad**
old - young	**North - South**

Cohesion. Cohesion refers to how well a story or article sticks together. This can be judged by seeing if the parts relate to the whole and how much one part is referred to by another part. For example, if one paragraph or sentence refers to another paragraph or sentence used earlier in the article or story. Also see Signal Words and Story Structures.

Dialogue. A dialogue is a conversation between characters in a story or play. *Example: He said, "I'll be home tonight".* Note: When you change speakers, each speaker is a new paragraph. Also note what is contained in a sentence (He said) and use of quotation marks.

Fact. A fact is a statement that can be proven. *Example: There are about four million children at each grade level.*

Fantasy. Fantasy is a story that has imagined characters, settings or other elements that could never really exist. *Example: Mickey Mouse or spiders that talk.*

118

Flashback. A break in the chronological sequence where an earlier incident is described.

Hyperbole. A hyperbole is an exaggeration. *Example: He must have been nine feet tall.*

Idiom. An expression that cannot be understood from the literal meaning of its worlds. *Example: Tom is barking up the wrong tree.*

Imagery. The author's use of description and words to create vivid pictures or images in the reader's mind. *Example: A blanket of soft snow covered the sleeping tractors.*

Irony. The use of tone, exaggeration or understatement to suggest the opposite of the literal meaning of the words used. *Example: I didn't mind waiting two hours; it was restful.* (Irony can be related to sarcasm).

Litotes. An understatement or assertion made by denying or negating its opposite. *Example: He wasn't unhappy about winning the bet.*

Metaphor. A metaphor is the comparison of two things without using the words "like" or "as." *Example: Habits are first cobwebs, then cables.* Metaphors can be larger ideas. *Example: Using a football game as a metaphor for the struggles in life.*
> **sense metaphor.** Relates one of the five senses to an object or situation. *Example: a cool reception.*

> **frozen metaphor.** A metaphor so frequently used that it has become an idiom or an expression with understood, but not literal, meaning. *Example: Head of the class.*

> **humanistic metaphor.** Gives inanimate objects human qualities or humans inanimate qualities. *Example: A user-friendly computer; her porcelain skin.*

> **inanimate metaphor.** Pairs the quality of an inanimate object with another inanimate object. *Example: The walls were paper thin.*

> **abstract metaphor.** Links an abstract concept with an object. *Example: Death is the pits.*

> **animal metaphor.** Associates the characteristics of an animal with a human or object. *Example: What a teddy bear he is!*

> **incarnation metaphor.** Links the attributes of a deceased person to another person or entity. *Example: He is a modern George Washington.* [Note: Similes are a type of metaphor.]

Metonymy. Metonymy is the use of a related word in place of what is really being talked about. *Example: "pen" instead of "writing" or "dry" instead of "thirsty".*

News Article. Articles in a newspaper often follow the old form that the 5 basic questions (Who? What? Why? When? Where?) are answered in the first sentence or at least in the first paragraph. This isn't always true, but it is a good starting place. Also, keep your paragraphs short and your information factual, not opinionated.

Onomatopoeia. Onomatopoeia are words in which the sounds suggest the meaning of the words. *Examples: Ouch, bang, bow wow, drip drip, oink, crash.*

Opinion. An opinion is a statement of someone's idea or feelings. An opinion cannot be proven. An opinion can be based on facts. *Example: George is the best candidate.* In a newspaper, editorials and signed columns are supposed to contain opinions.

Personification. Linking a human quality or ability to an animal, object or idea is called personification. *Examples: The wind whispered through the night. Friendly computers.*

Point of view. Point of view refers to how a story is narrated. If a story is narrated from the first person point of view, the narrator is a character in the story and uses the first person pronouns I, me, mine, we, and our. If the story is narrated from the third person point of view, the narrator is not part of the story and uses the third person pronouns he, him, she, her, them.

Prediction. The use of facts in the story and other information you know about the world to guess what will happen is making a prediction. *Example: The world will be overcrowded in 2040.*

Setting. The time and place in which the story happens is called the setting. *Example: She lived in England in the last century.*

Signal Words. These words refer to the story structure or cohesion, but more specifically, they tell the reader something is coming up, or that the next part of writing is somehow related. Here are some specific kinds of Signal Words:

1. **Continuation Signals.** *Examples: and, in addition, also.*
2. **Change of Direction Signals.** *Examples: but, however, in contrast.*
3. **Sequence Signals.** *Examples: next, second, since, later.*
4. **Illustration Signals.** *Examples: for example, to illustrate, such as.*
5. **Emphasis Signals.** *Examples: remember that, the key feature, most important.*
6. **Cause, Condition or Result Signals.** *Examples: if, while, due to, because.*

7. **Spatial Signals.** *Examples: under, between, on, close to.*
8. **Comparison-contrast Signals.** *Examples: less than, different from, same.*
9. **Conclusion Signals.** *Examples: in conclusion, in summary, therefore.*
10. **Fuzz Signals.** *Examples: if, maybe, could, looks like, probably.*
11. **Nonword Emphasis Signals.** *Examples: Exclamation point, underline, subheads.*

Simile. A simile is a comparison of two things using the words "like" or "as." *Example: She felt as limp as a rag doll.* [Similes are a type of metaphor. See metaphor for types.]

Story Structures. There are a lot of ways to structure stories. Here is a short list of some different kinds of story structures:

1. **cause and effect**
2. **sequence or chronological order**
3. **comparison or contrast**
4. **statements and conclusions**
5. **conflict and resolution**
6. **description**
7. **main idea and detail**
8. **problem and solution**
9. **theme, essay, academic discussion of a topic**
10. **news article**
11. **mystery story – surprise ending**

Synonyms. A synonym is a word or phrase (short group of words) that mean the same or about the same as another word. For example, "like" and "enjoy" mean about the same thing in some sentences. However, most words have several meanings, so be sure that you use a synonym that means what you want to say. For example, here is a plain sentence: He said, "She likes me." Here is a similar sentence with some synonyms: The big guy whispered, "She really enjoys my company." Here are a few synonyms:

> **night = evening, dark, after sunset**
> **boy = guy, fellow, young man, child, student**
> **said = yelled, asked, whispered, called**
> **go = leave, depart, run away, move**

Many dictionaries have synonyms as part of the definition or in a separate list, and there are whole books of synonyms some of which are called a "thesaurus".

TEACHING SUGGESTIONS

You can greatly aid the effectiveness of this book if you explain each part of it carefully and provide drills on usage. Here are some suggested drills that will enhance skills they need to really use this book.

Most of the drills can be done with the whole class or a smaller group, or even individual tutoring. They can be oral or written. Make up many more of your own sample questions. Take several days or many days to do these familiarization drills. Many of the drills, or sections of this book, suggest whole lessons, or at least more explanation and teaching.

Students should try to find the answers in the book. The object of the lesson, or preferably lessons, is to learn to use the Beginning Writers Manual as a reference book. Students are not expected to know the answers but they are expected to learn where to find the answers.

Guide Letters
Spelling Check
Pages 9 - 66

Using just the letters at the top of the page, quickly find just the page on which each of the following words are located. Give the page number.

wheel   obtain   February

(Note for this drill, don't take time to find the word, the purpose is to learn to use the guide letters at the top of the page).

Alphabetization
Spelling Check
Pages 9 - 66

Now find the following words, using first the guide letters at the top of the page, then the two letter word group heading in the page. Give the word just before each.

eagle   Sweden   polar

Variant Forms
Spelling Check
Pages 9 - 66

What other word forms are in the word list for each of these base words?

beg   Spain   vote

Homophones
Spelling Check
Pages 9 - 66
   What other words have the same sound but different meanings as each of these words?
   for   **weigh**   **do**

Capitalization
Pages 74 - 75
   Name three kinds of words that need to be written with a capital letter.

Punctuation
Pages 76 - 77
   What are 3 times you need to use a period?

Apostrophe
Pages 78 - 79
   What are the 3 main different uses of an apostrophe?

Abbreviations
Pages 80 - 83
   What are the abbreviations for each of the following?
   Maine   **A married woman**   **Monday**
   foot   **centimeter**   **adverb**

Letter Forms
Pages 96 - 97
   How does a business letter differ from a friendly letter?

Phonics
Pages 69 - 73
   What are three ways the Long A sound can be spelled?

Spelling Rules
Plurals
Pages 67 - 68
   How do you spell the plural of "fox", "candy", "knife"?

Spelling Rules
Suffixes
Pages 67 - 68
   Watch your spelling and add the following suffixes to the base word.
   nose + y   **marry + ed**   **hit + ing**

Grammar
Sentences
Pages 84 - 87
   Take this sentence, " I can do my homework." and change it into a negative sentence.
   Now change it into a question.
   Finally, change it into passive voice.

Grammar
Verbs
Pages 89 - 92
   Correct the following verb errors:
   She sing very well.
   She sing yesterday.
   She sing tomorrow.
   She sing in the shower now.

Grammar
Parts of Speech
Pages 93 - 94
   What is the Part Of Speech for each of the following words:
   man   **run**   **beautiful**
   beautifully   **and**   **he**

Types of Writing
Page 95
   Name 3 different types of writing.

Journal Keeping
Pages 100 - 101
   Name 3 different things you might write about in your journal.

Book Report
Pages 98 - 99
   How does a Book Report Form differ from a Story Map form?

Graphs
Pages 102 - 103
   Name 3 types of graphs that can show numerical (quantitative) data.

Vocabulary Improvement
Page 104
   What are 3 ways to improve your vocabulary?

Writing Process
Pages 105 - 111
    What are the four Stages in the writing process?

Proofreading Symbols
Page 112
    What is the symbol for making a new paragraph?

Story Starters
Page 113 - 116
        Give one of each of the following:
        Interesting Titles   Opening Sentences
        Great Questions   Story Enders

Literary Terms
Pages 117 - 121
        Give your own example for each of the following terms:
        Alliteration   contraction   antonym
        hyperbole   idiom   metaphor

Personal Spelling List
Pages 122 - 126
    Name three kinds of words you should add to your personal
spelling list.

These drills have two main purposes. The first is to familiarize your students
with the contents of the book and where they are located. The second is to develop
speed in locating the information.

The first few drills which involve alphabetization require a lot of practice. Drill
your students several times a week for several weeks to develop speed and accuracy.
Give extra drills to slower students. Use lavish praise or other rewards for students
who are fastest, most accurate, have just caught on, or who are making progress.

Teach to transfer the skills learned in the drills to real life situations. For
example, if during a writing exercise a student asks you how to spell a word, you ask
him to look it up in the book. If a student turns in a paper with spelling errors, ask
him to look up the incorrect word. If a student turns in a paper with incorrect
punctuation or a letter in a poor form, refer him or her to this book for correct
information.

Each of the sections of the Beginning Writers Manual provide the content for
many lessons. For example, the Punctuation section suggests lessons on comma use
or apostrophe use. The section on Spelling Rules suggests lessons on spelling of
plurals or doubling the final letter when adding a suffix.

Finally, tell your students that even very experienced writers have to look up the
spelling of some words or the proper punctuation. Everybody who writes should use
reference works and this is a fine one to start with.

PERSONAL SPELLING LIST

A lot of good writers keep a Personal Spelling List. Just writing the word in a Personal Spelling List will help you to learn it, but the real time saver is that the next time you need to look up a word, it is much faster and easier to find it in a Personal Spelling List.

This list is made up of: 1. Words that they have had to look up in a dictionary. 2. Words that they frequently misspell. 3. Names of people, cities, and things not easily found in a dictionary or Spelling Checker list. 4. Words unique to a subject, like biology, music, sports. 5. Foreign words and phrases.

A

B

C

D

E

F

G

H

I

J _____   _____   _____

_____   _____   _____

K _____   _____   _____

_____   _____   _____

L _____   _____   _____

_____   _____   _____

_____   _____   _____

_____   _____   _____

_____   _____   _____

_____   _____   _____

M _____   _____   _____

_____   _____   _____

_____   _____   _____

_____   _____   _____

_____   _____   _____

_____   _____   _____

N _____   _____   _____

_____   _____   _____

O _____   _____   _____

_____   _____   _____

_____   _____   _____

Personal Spelling List

P

Q

R

S

T

129

U

V

W

X

Y

Z

INDEX

Index